THE ENTREPRENEURIAL FACTOR IN ECONOMIC GROWTH

Also by Harold Lydall

THE STRUCTURE OF EARNINGS
A THEORY OF INCOME DISTRIBUTION
YUGOSLAV SOCIALISM: Theory and Practice
YUGOSLAVIA IN CRISIS

The Entrepreneurial Factor in Economic Growth

Harold Lydall

M

First published 1992 by
MACMILLAN ACADEMIC AND PROFESSIONAL LTD
Houndmills, Basingstoke, Hampshire RG21 2XS
and London
Companies and representatives
throughout the world

ISBN 0–333–56923–7 hardcover

A catalogue record for this book is available
from the British Library.

Typeset by Typeset Gallery, Malaysia
Printed in Hong Kong

Contents

Preface

The ideas presented in this book have matured slowly – far too slowly – over a long period of time. Three strands of thought have come together. The first concerns the theory of the firm; more specifically, the concept of freedom of entry. I first attempted to clarify this in an article in *Oxford Economic Papers* in October 1955. Five years later, when I was working temporarily in India, I continued to think about the same problem, but in a more practical context, when I joined with P. N. Dhar in writing a short book on the role of small enterprises in Indian economic development. Meanwhile, I had been doing a good deal of work on the distribution of income; and this became the second strand. The work culminated in a major study of the structure of earnings, in the course of which I came to the conclusion that one of the important factors which determines the final distribution of earned income is a personal quality of 'drive', or 'determination'. Subsequently, I suggested that this quality should be called 'the D-Factor'. Although I did not recognize it at the time, it is clear that this is one of the most important qualities, if not the most important quality, possessed by successful entrepreneurs. The third strand arose out of my more recent researches into the economic system of communist Yugoslavia, from which I learned that the greatest deficiency in that system is the shortage of good entrepreneurs.

If it seems absurd that it has taken me nearly forty years to become convinced that the key factor in economic development is entrepreneurship, I can only offer the defence that there are still many economists – perhaps even the majority – who are not yet convinced of the same elementary truth. That is the reason why I have written this book.

I wish to acknowledge my indebtedness to the Oxford University Institute of Economics and Statistics for the use of their excellent library and photocopying facilities. My connection with the Institute started more than forty years ago and continues, in a small way, even now.

HAROLD LYDALL

1 The Nature of the Problem

Three great facts are largely ignored in standard economic theory. The first is that the predominant part of the rapid technical progress of the past two and half centuries has been generated within enterprises. Standard economic theory assumes that technology is 'given', coming from outside industry. Yet even the most superficial acquaintance with actual events demonstrates that this is not the case. While scientific advance has played a crucial role in many fields, it has never been a sufficient condition for technical progress; and in many cases, especially in earlier centuries, it was not even a necessary condition.[1] If technology were really 'given', it would be impossible to understand why it is not used equally by all countries. If science were the sole source of technology, one might ask why the Soviet Union, which has devoted enormous resources to science, persistently lags behind in technical development (except perhaps in the military field). Why does Japan, which devotes much less resources to science, now lead the world in many fields of technology? Why is Britain, with so many Nobel prizes to its credit, so technically unprogressive?

The second great fact relates to the model of perfect competition, which is the foundation stone of standard economic theory. Everyone knows, or should know, that perfect competition implies perfect knowledge – of prices, technology, and the future. And everyone also knows that such knowledge does not exist, indeed could not exist. But the model of perfect competition goes on, its incompatibility with known facts seeming to raise no serious doubts about its validity.

Thirdly, it is self-evident that capital and labour do not combine spontaneously to produce goods and services. Someone has to make the necessary decisions about how these factors should be combined, and what goods or services should be produced. The name of that person is the entrepreneur. But his role in the production process is almost entirely ignored. Many economic texts do not even mention him; and only in very rare cases is his role discussed.

Each of these three contradictions between well-known facts and the content of economic theory can be traced to a single origin: an unwillingness to recognize the role of the entrepreneur. There could be a number of reasons for that attitude. But I think that the dominant one is the incompatibility of entrepreneurship with perfect competition. To give proper attention to the role of entrepreneurship would entail the abandonment of the model of perfect competition, in the development of which so much has been invested.

A PRELIMINARY VIEW OF THE STRENGTHS AND WEAKNESSES OF PERFECT COMPETITION

It is easy to see why economists are attracted by the model of perfect competition. In the first place, it provides a rational explanation for the 'laws of supply and demand', which have constituted a basic building block of economic theory since the time of Adam Smith. Secondly, the model yields, in principle, clear and precise forecasts of equilibrium prices. Thirdly, the model purports to account for a wide range of other economic phenomena, including the structure of output, and the level and distribution of income. Fourthly, perfect competition seems to be a necessary (and sufficient) condition for the existence of a general Pareto-optimal equilibrium, which has important welfare connotations. Finally, and perhaps most important of all, the model of perfect competition lends itself well to the application of the differential calculus, and has thus done more than anything else to open the door to the widespread use of mathematics in economics.

But these advantages of the model of perfect competition are not a sufficient justification for its acceptance as the dominant model in economics. Apart from the perfect knowledge requirement already referred to, perfect competition is based on a number of other assumptions which are clearly unsatisfactory; and the predictions of the model are in several respects sharply in conflict with observed facts. These weaknesses will be examined in detail in Chapter 2. But it will be useful to give a brief summary at this point.

In order to avoid misunderstanding, it should be made clear that it will not be suggested in this book that the perfect competition model has *no* application at all in a modern industrialized economy. The model provides an approximate explanation of short-run adjustments in industries producing some primary products, and in a similar manner for some personal services, as well as in parts of the building industry in which small firms predominate. But for the great bulk of the economy the predictions of the competitive model are not verified. Relative prices are more stable than they would be under perfect competition, and most short-run adjustments to changes in demand conditions are made through changes in outputs, with little or no changes in prices.

The behaviour of factor markets is generally also not in accord with the predictions of the perfect competition model. Wages are largely fixed by collective bargaining, administrative regulation, or by reference to 'custom'. The unemployed do not compete significantly with those in employment, and relative wages are not sensitive to the levels of unemployment of different industries or skills. In the capital market it has never been possible for a borrower to obtain as much finance as he wishes at the 'going' rate of interest, and there is always a queue, whether open or hidden, of unsatisfied borrowers. The level and structure of interest rates are largely determined by administrative or institutional decisions.

As already mentioned, a crucial assumption of the perfect competition model is that technology is a free good. This is what is meant by the standard assumption of an objectively given production function. Simple predictions from that assumption would include (1) that there will be no such phenomenon as 'X-inefficiency', (2) that there will be no foreign direct investment, and (3) that there will be no demand from poorer countries for institutionally arranged 'technical transfer'. Since all these predictions are false, the assumption of 'given' technology must be rejected; and this knocks away one of the foundations of the perfect competition model.

Some other assumptions of the perfect competition model are more often implicit than explicit. One of these is the assumption that there are no time lags in adjustments of supply. In the standard diagram of supply and demand, in which the vertical axis is labelled 'price' and the horizontal axis 'quantity', it is implicitly assumed that today's output can be adjusted to today's price. Only if this were so, would the price move immediately towards equilibrium. In fact, of course, except in the provision of some personal services, today's output (even in the 'short run') is the result of decisions taken many weeks or months ago. In most cases, today's price can have little or no effect on today's output. In an industry which conforms to the perfect competition model in all respects other than the absence of time lags in adjustment, changes in demand or supply conditions are likely to produce a 'cobweb' rather than a smooth movement towards equilibrium. The rarity of cobweb patterns of adjustment in modern industries is evidence that these industries are not operating under conditions of perfect competition. A further implication of the assumption that there are no time lags of adjustment is that the perfect competition model is unable to offer any coherent account of the behaviour of investment.

Since the perfect competition model works only under static conditions, i.e. in the absence of time lags, the use of the model tends to divert attention from the effects of expectations on economic behaviour. Firms are often assumed to behave in a short-sighted manner, and the use of this assumption generates predictions which are patently absurd. The perfect competition model is unable to account for speculation or, more generally, for expectation-influenced behaviour. As a consequence, it can offer no coherent explanation of the business cycle or of many of the fluctuations in exchange rates. Almost the whole of the Keynesian theory of employment is inconsistent with perfect competition.

Although some of the weaknesses of the model of perfect competition mentioned above relate to the failure of its predictions, others relate to the lack of realism of its assumptions. Since inclusion of the latter group will encounter objections from the adherents of Friedman's interpretation of 'positive economics', it is necessary at this point to give attention to some questions of methodology.

SOME QUESTIONS OF METHODOLOGY

The validity of a theoretical model can be assessed by scrutinizing its assumptions, its logic, or its predictions; or, better still, by scrutinizing all three. Some methodological confusion has been generated by the well-known thesis of Milton Friedman that the realism of assumptions is irrelevant to the validity of a theory, and that, while correct logic is important, the crucial (and only ultimate) criterion for assessing the acceptability of a theory is the accuracy of its predictions.[2] Is this view acceptable?

The structure of a theoretical model, at least in economics, seems always to consist of four components. First, there are environmental assumptions. Although these may be of many different sorts, an example of a common environmental assumption in economics is that we are considering a market economy, in which people are free to make their own decisions about 'economic' matters, such as consumption, production, and trade. Secondly, there are behavioural assumptions, such as the assumption that people are rational utility-maximizers. Thirdly, there is the logical structure of the model, which combines the two kinds of assumptions to generate predictions about the behaviour of the given economy. This logical structure can often be most efficiently checked with the help of mathematics. Finally, there are the predictions themselves, which can be tested by empirical observations. These may be of various kinds, ranging from previous experience, or 'common sense', to new measurements and the use of econometric methods.

Friedman's criticism in the essay referred to in footnote 2 above was directed mainly at economists who, on the basis of the replies given by businessmen in surveys, questioned the realism of the profit-maximizing assumption. Since these replies suggested that businessmen do not calculate marginal revenue and marginal cost, it was argued that businessmen's decisions are not primarily directed towards maximizing profits. It was open to Friedman to argue that asking people about their motives or other mental processes is a naive, and often unreliable, method of discovering the character of such psychological phenomena. However, he chose to challenge the conclusions drawn from these surveys by a much stronger argument based on methodological principle. First, he maintained that theoretical assumptions, which should preferably be simple, can never be 'realistic', because reality is so complex that these assumptions can never be *descriptively* accurate. Secondly, he argued that the usefulness of such assumptions can be assessed only by testing the predictions of the model, taken as a whole, against empirical observations.

Now the first of Friedman's methodological objections is the result of verbal confusion. No one, to my knowledge, has ever suggested that theoretical assumptions should be 'descriptive' in the sense that they provide a complete inventory of the whole environment, or that they cover all aspects of human behaviour that might conceivably influence the outcome of the model. When people talk about the 'realism' of an assumption they do not mean that the assumption is a comprehensive description of reality. In the case of environmental assumptions, they mean that the model is designed to work only within the specified environment. For example, the model of perfect competition is not designed to work in a command economy, or when the industry in question is a monopoly. Although in either of these cases the environment will have many other characteristics, it is usually quite easy to ascertain whether the environmental assumptions required for perfect competition are present or not.

In the case of behavioural assumptions, the position is somewhat different. Behavioural assumptions are not definitions of the circumstances in which the model is designed to work, but general assumptions about the behavioural tendencies of entities (in economics, people, or organizations), which may operate in a wide variety of environments. These tendencies cannot usually be observed directly. They can be verified or falsified only indirectly, by observing predictions derived from them. But these predictions can be of many different kinds. The utility-maximizing assumption can be tested by asking people questions about their responses to changes in relative prices. It can also be tested by observing people in an experimental environment. Or it can be tested, along with all the other components of the neoclassical model, by means of aggregate data on market behaviour. There is no special reason for giving preference to the last kind of test. Indeed, because this is a test of *all* the components of the model simultaneously, it does not discriminate between those components. It may well be naive to ask people about their motives, but there are other methods of testing the 'realism' of behavioural components without relying solely on a comprehensive test of the whole model.

What do we do if we find that one component of a model fails the test of realism by some simple test of its predictions, even when the predictions of the model as a whole are reasonably well confirmed by observation? It would surely be sensible to be concerned by the weakness of that component. A car may operate successfully in many circumstances with a weak battery; but eventually the day will come when the driver is stranded, and it would be better if he were to check his battery from time to time. From a scientific point of view, moreover, it is unacceptable to put one's faith in a model, even when it normally 'works', if one knows that one of its assumptions is completely unrealistic. Friedman's example of a tree whose leaves are assumed to move round the trunk in order to face the sun is a case in point. This assumption may provide a reasonably good explanation of the greater density of leaves on the sunny side. But observation of the behaviour of the leaves (on the basis of the prediction that, if the leaves move, it should be possible to see them move) will leave no doubt that the assumption is false, and that the model needs to be amended.

For the case of the apparently non-profit-maximizing businessmen Friedman offered an ingenious alternative theory to reconcile their introspective statements with their actual behaviour. Under competitive conditions, 'natural selection' will ensure that only successful businesses will survive. The surviving businesses will be making profits, or at least not making losses. So competition ensures that profits are maximized, irrespective of the subjective intentions of businessmen. But the last conclusion does not follow. If, as this theory implies, there is a dispersion of business ability (or at least of success), the theory predicts that no loss-making businesses will survive. But it does not predict that each successful business is making its maximum profit, i.e. that it is operating at its most efficient scale, at minimum cost, and so forth. Yet this kind of prediction is needed in order to prove that perfect competition is allocationally efficient (and also 'X-efficient'). Unless businessmen are rational profit-maximizers (and have the necessary information to achieve that result), none of the reassuring theorems of neoclassical economics is valid.

There is a further consideration that cannot be overlooked. It is a fundamental assumption of neoclassical theory that people in a market economy are 'economic men', or rational utility-maximizers. Without that assumption it would be impossible to provide a coherent theory of consumer choice, since we cannot in this case resort to the assumption that 'natural selection' eliminates consumers who do not behave 'as if' they were utility-maximizers. It would be very awkward, to say the least, to make use of the utility-maximizing assumption in some parts of economic theory and to discard it in other parts. Such inconsistency of assumptions within a single field of study would pose a threat to the reliability of the whole set of theories.

Instead of disbelieving what businessmen say about their motives or objectives, it would be better to look carefully at the orthodox theoretical model and consider whether there may be some defects in it, which account for differences between the predicted replies of businessmen to questions about their objectives and their actual replies. A suggested alternative theory, which is compatible with such survey information, will be presented in Chapter 4.

Despite these criticisms of Friedman's thesis about the irrelevance of the realism of assumptions, there can be no doubt that the crucial ultimate test of any theory is the coincidence of its predictions with observed facts, provided, of course, that the observations are made under environmental conditions corresponding at least 'approximately' to those prescribed in the environmental assumptions. One of the environmental assumptions of perfect competition is that there are numerous buyers and sellers of any product, none of whom has a large share of the market. It would, therefore, be inappropriate to test the predictions of the perfect competition model in a market in which each producer offered for sale a product with significantly different characteristics.

Friedman has also argued that, although a particular environmental (or behavioural) assumption is not *strictly* true, it may be 'near enough' true if it yields predictions which are approximately confirmed by experience. This argument is acceptable up to a point. No scientist, especially no social scientist, normally expects his environmental assumptions to be completely or exactly fulfilled when he is making an empirical test of his theory. If the predictions of his theory are 'largely' confirmed by empirical tests, the scientist's confidence in the validity of his theory will not be shaken by his knowledge that some of his environmental assumptions are 'slightly' unrealistic. This is an area in which the theorist's judgement (and the judgement of his critics) is bound to have a considerable influence. In sciences in which the environment can be tightly controlled, such as some of the natural sciences, this problem is minimized. In the social sciences, however, we are not in such a fortunate position; and there will always be room for debate about the realism of the environmental assumptions of any particular model. Nevertheless, it is right that the main emphasis in such debates should be put on the accuracy of predictions.

PLAN OF FURTHER DISCUSSION

Despite its obvious deficiencies, the perfect competition model still holds the centre of the field. Previous efforts to replace it, especially by the development of the theory of imperfect or monopolistic competition, have been largely unsuccessful. The reason, it seems, is that this latter theory is a halfway house, a partial attempt to revise the perfect competition model while continuing to make use of a number of its invalid assumptions. These assumptions include 'given' technology, 'free entry', and the absence of expectation-influenced behaviour.

But perfect competition can be driven from its dominant position in economic theory only if there is a better alternative theory of competition, a theory that is more appropriate to conditions in modern industrialized economies. Suggestions for such a theory will be presented in subsequent chapters. For reasons that will be given later, this alternative theory will be described as an 'entrepreneurial' theory of competition. In Chapter 2 we shall examine in more detail the defects of the perfect competition model, and in particular its failure to predict observed phenomena. In Chapter 3 we shall make a first step towards revising the model of perfect competition, by considering the effects of combining the assumptions of perfect competition in product markets with imperfections in the supplies of technology and the factors of production. This set of conditions will be described as 'semi-perfect' competition. Chapter 4 will then extend the discussion to include the well-known condition of imperfect competition in product markets; and a model will be constructed to account for the observed behaviour of firms when there are imperfections in all markets – for products, technology, and the factors of production. This model, which will be called 'fixprice' competition, provides even wider scope for the activities of entrepreneurs. But, before proceeding to a closer analysis of the role of entrepreneurs, we consider in Chapter 5 an interesting, although subsidiary, question. This is a comparison of the optimality of three kinds of competition: perfect, semi-perfect, and fixprice. Chapter 6 is then devoted to the question of the role of the entrepreneur; and Chapter 7 to the factors influencing the supply of entrepreneurs. Finally, in Chapter 8 some wider issues are raised, including the effects of international trade, and the implications of our microeconomic model for the aggregate distribution of income. This chapter also includes a brief discussion of the role of government, and of the reasons for the poor performance of economic systems which have transferred most economic decisions from private entrepreneurs to the state.

2 Perfect Competition

This chapter will contain a more detailed assessment of the model of perfect competition. We shall start by considering the necessary (and sufficient) assumptions of the model, some of which are usually explicit while others are only implicit. We shall then proceed to appraise the model under three headings: the realism of its assumptions; its logical structure; and the verification of its predictions.

THE ASSUMPTIONS OF THE MODEL

In most textbooks, or even in monographs about price theory, the list of assumptions which are said to be required for the model of perfect competition is somewhat cursory. The requirement given most emphasis is that the number of buyers and sellers of a product must be large, and that none of them has an excessive share of the market. This assumption may also be expressed by the proposition that the elasticity of demand for the product of each firm is, for practical purposes, infinite, as is the elasticity of supply of the same product to each consumer. In these circumstances, producers and consumers will adjust their supply and demand decisions to 'given' market prices. This, of course, implies that all producers and consumers have accurate knowledge of those prices, and of the qualities of the goods or services offered for sale.

Similar conditions are assumed to operate in the markets for the factors of production. But, since most factors of production are hired rather than bought, some further assumptions are required to ensure that these markets achieve the required degree of perfection. For example, it must be assumed that the qualities of hired factors are not affected in unpredictable ways by the experience of being hired, and can instantly be returned intact to the market if no longer needed. Otherwise both the prices and qualities of particular units of the factors would be subject to some uncertainty, which is inconsistent with the model. In the case of labour, it is also implicitly assumed that a hired worker will always perform at the level of efficiency expected by the employer at the time of making the contract. Workers, in other words, are similar to machines, which can be expected to behave according to their technical specifications.

The demands of consumers are assumed to be subject to the 'law of diminishing marginal utility', while on the supply side firms are assumed to be operating in the short run under conditions of decreasing marginal product of each factor and increasing marginal cost of output. On the assumption of 'free entry', in the long run all firms making the same product will be of identical size, and changes in long-run supply will be brought about by increasing or reducing the number of such firms. This means that, except when there is a shortage of specific factors needed to produce a product, the long-run elasticity of supply of output will be close to infinite.

The 'free entry' assumption implies not only that there are no obstacles to entry but that potential new entrants have all the necessary information to take advantage of that freedom. This means, in particular, that they must have free access to all the relevant technology, i.e. that technology must be 'given'. In addition, if the market for any product is to move fairly smoothly towards long-run equilibrium, potential new entrants must be able to make fairly accurate estimates of the product's long-run equilibrium price. Indeed, strictly speaking, potential new entrants need to know in advance what prices will be ruling during the whole lifetime of their investment.

Although these seem to be the necessary (and sufficient) conditions for the operation of the model of perfect competition, one must recognize that, since the model has been used and developed over a long period of time, it is possible that some of its hidden assumptions have been omitted. If we leave aside this possibility, we may summarize the necessary and sufficient assumptions for perfect competition as follows:

1. The general environment is a 'market economy' with private (or at least decentralized) ownership of the factors of production. Individuals and firms are free to trade goods and services, and to hire factors of production, with the aim of maximizing their incomes or levels of utility.

2. In the market for each product or factor of production both buyers and sellers can costlessly (or at least cheaply) obtain information about the prices at which the product or factor is currently being offered for sale or hire. Potential traders can also costlessly or cheaply obtain accurate information about the qualities of available products and factors.
3. In each market there are considerable numbers of independent buyers and sellers, who compete with one another to obtain the prices most favourable to them. None has an excessive share of the market.
4. The demand of individual consumers for almost all products is subject to the 'law of diminishing marginal utility'; and, at least in expansion, the short-run marginal cost of production of every product in every firm is upward-sloping.
5. At a given moment of time, knowledge of the range of alternative technologies for producing a particular product is freely available to all potential producers of the product (in effect, to the whole population).
6. There are no legal obstacles to the entry of new producers, nor to the exit of existing producers.
7. When actual or potential producers are considering possible investment projects, they can fairly easily make accurate estimates of the prices which will be ruling in the market during the expected life of such investments.

THE REALISM OF THE ASSUMPTIONS

It is reasonably easy to verify whether Assumption 1 (a market economy) is satisfied in any particular case. Although it is never completely satisfied, economists have usually been prepared to overlook minor deviations from this assumption. It would, however, be unrealistic to make use of the model of perfect competition in an economy in which more than half of the national product was centrally planned, or where free markets for labour or capital were lacking.

The major difficulty with Assumption 2 is the frequent absence of accurate information about the qualities of available factors of production. On the side of employers, there is often much uncertainty about the characteristics of possible new employees, and both employers and employees may have difficulty in ensuring that the other side carries out the terms of the (explicit or implicit) contract of employment. The performance of workers varies considerably from one firm to another, and much of this variation seems to be the result of differences in the firm's methods of organization and motivation. Under these conditions, it is not realistic to assume that all technology is 'given', nor that there is a highly elastic supply of new firms of equal efficiency.

Similar problems arise in the case of capital. Because most capital is lent in the form of money, rather than in the form of specific capital goods, the lenders are subject to considerable uncertainty about the prospects of receiving their capital back at the end of the loan. In other words, potential lenders are uncertain about the 'quality' of the capital which they are being asked to lend. Because of this inevitable degree of uncertainty in the capital market, it is unrealistic to assume that the supply of capital under perfect competition is infinitely elastic to individual borrowers.

In modern economies, Assumption 3 is not satisfied in most industries producing manufactures and services, and even in some primary industries. There are statutory monopolies in some cases, but over most of the field there is systematic product differentiation. Product differentiation leads to forms of behaviour quite different from those predicted by the model of perfect competition. (As a test, consider how many goods or services in such economies are sold by auction.) It has long been recognized that imperfect competition in product markets requires a different model. But the standard model of imperfect competition is unsatisfactory, as will be explained in detail in Chapter 4.

Assumption 4 is realistic. Indeed, it seems to be part of the 'laws of nature', of man and of matter. It is, therefore, an assumption which, like Assumption 1, must be included in any model of a market economy.

Assumption 5, on the other hand, is completely unrealistic. Technology is not a free good, because much of technical knowledge is internal to the firm and consequently privately owned. This question will be examined fully in Chapter 3, where its implications for an alternative model of competition will also be developed.

Assumption 6 is usually realistic for most privately-owned industries in a market economy. It is, of course, violated whenever there are legally protected private or public monopolies.

Assumption 7 is, of course, absurd. It is not merely unrealistic but logically inconsistent with the previous assumptions. For example, if every potential entrant thought that he knew for certain that the future equilibrium price of a product would be higher than the present one, and if technology was a free good, there would be such an inrush of new entrants that the long-run price would fall rather than rise. Yet Assumption 7 is necessary if perfect competition is to generate a state of long-run equilibrium. This combination of necessity and absurdity creates insoluble problems for the model, and points to its fundamental weakness, which is its inability to incorporate time (and hence uncertainty).

THE LOGICAL STRUCTURE OF THE MODEL

A major logical problem for the model of perfect competition is how to allow for the existence of time. Since production takes time, and investment decisions are made with a view to future yields, the problem of time lags between decisions and outcomes cannot be avoided in any model which purports to account for the behaviour of a real economy. Three kinds of attempt have been made to solve this problem.

The first, which is not really a solution of the problem but rather an evasion, is the static model. In this model time lags, and hence time itself, are assumed out of existence.[1] All potential buyers and sellers are assumed to bring their goods or services to market, to submit them to an auctioning process which brings about an equality of supply and demand for all goods and services at an equilibrium set of prices, and then to exchange at those prices. Such a model provides a reasonable interpretation of a market for *perishable* goods and personal services, where time lags in both production and consumption can be ignored. But it cannot be applied to a market for storable goods, the prices of which are bound to be influenced by expectations of future prices. The expected future prices of such goods will be influenced by, among other things, the expected future level of production of such goods; and the expectations of both potential buyers and sellers about this matter are subject to many kinds of uncertainty, including uncertainty about expected changes in natural conditions, in technology, in relative prices (of all goods and services), and in the responses of other potential producers to their own expectations on all these points. In other words, the model excludes both time lags in production and the influence of speculation, and for these reasons it is not a very useful model for a modern industrialized economy.

An even more acute problem for the static model is how to account for investment decisions, and hence to establish the possibility of *long-run* equilibrium. Since investments, by the definition of the term, are made with a view to their future yields, it is impossible to incorporate investment decisions in a static model unless one makes the assumption that their future yields are known with certainty. But this is not only a practical but also a logical impossibility. For an individual investor to have certain knowledge of the future yields of a specific investment project he would need to know with certainty how other potential investors were likely to behave. And this is a kind of knowledge which is incompatible with a basic assumption of the model, that all firms act independently and have no prior knowledge of how their competitors will behave.

A second attempted solution to the problem of incorporating time in the model of perfect competition is the stationary state assumption. In this case, time is allowed to exist; but it is made irrelevant by the assumption that nothing ever changes. If nothing ever changes, and people know it to be so, their expectations will be determinate and certain: they will be determined by current experience. In that case, no difficulty arises from the existence of time lags in production. Expected prices will be equal to current prices, and production decisions made on that basis will turn out to be correct. Equilibrium, once attained, will be self-perpetuating. But the cost of making this assumption is that the model cannot be used to account for changes in tastes, technology, or the supplies of the factors of production.

Economics is reduced to a beautiful theorem which can never tell us anything about the real world.

A third attempted solution to the problem is the Arrow-Debreu model.[2] In this model it assumed that in year 0 everyone offers to make sets of alternative contracts for all kinds of economic transactions in the future, where each set of contracts is conditional on the existence on a future date of a particular 'state of the world'. A 'state of the world' is a detailed description of endowments and production possibilities for every person and firm assumed to be in existence on the future date. A general equilibrium is then established, by Walrasian methods, for each alternative set of contracts. All that would then remain to do would be to ascertain on the given future date what was the state of the world, since this would determine which equilibrium was applicable.

There are several objections to this 'solution' of the problem of time. On a practical level, it would be inconceivable that everyone would have sufficient knowledge, or time, to draw up such a vast number of hypothetical contracts. But the logical objections to this model are more fundamental. In the first place, any contract dependent for its fulfilment on investment decisions (which means in practice virtually all contracts) would need to be made contingent on the state of the world not only on one future date, but on a series of future dates. Since it would not be until the end of that period that everyone would know what set of contracts was in force, uncertainty and disequilibrium would continue to exist. Secondly, since public information is not available about the endowments and production possibilities of persons and firms, it would be impossible to discover the precise 'state of the world', even on a single date. Thirdly, production possibilities depend on the state of technical knowledge, the future development of which cannot be described in advance, even in the imagination. It would be impossible, therefore, to draw up an exhaustive set of hypothetical contracts, contingent on alternative assumptions about production possibilities, when all possible forms of technology could not be specified.

Thus, all attempts to 'abstract from' or to 'endogenize' time have so far proved to be logically impossible (as well, of course, as being both remote from the real world and operationally sterile). The fundamental reason for this failure is that time means change, and change means uncertainty. But the model of perfect competition can work only in conditions of certainty. Hence it is incompatible with time. It is a logically inconsistent structure; and for this reason alone it cannot serve as a general theory of market behaviour, let alone as a theory of general equilibrium.

PREDICTIONS OF THE MODEL

The following are some of the predictions of the model of perfect competition that are partially or completely falsified in the modern world:

1. According to the model, equilibrium prices adjust to changes in exogenous conditions. They do not fluctuate around the new equilibrium; nor do they show a tendency to cumulative deviation. But fluctuations, which are sometimes of a wide amplitude and extending over several years, are frequently found in the prices of primary products. Although these fluctuations are usually started by changes in exogenous factors, they continue for a considerable time after the exogenous changes have ceased. These fluctuations seem to be partly the result of speculative activity; but they are mainly caused by the difficulty of making smooth adjustments from one equilibrium position to another in industries in which substantial production time lags are combined with highly competitive markets. Speculative activity also produces wide fluctuations in the prices of shares and other assets, especially private housing, and in the exchange values of currencies.
2. The model predicts that, when the demand for a good increases, its price will increase in the short run, and *vice versa*. While this pattern is still dominant for many primary products, for house construction and repair, for existing assets generally, and in a few other cases, for most modern industry and services the pattern of response is quite different. When demand for manufactured product *X* increases, the producers respond by increasing their sales at the same price, and *vice versa*. The prices of such products change, in general, only when their input costs of labour or materials

change. By way of exception, if an increase in demand is very large and persistent, there may be a slight tendency to increase prices, or to reduce quality of service; but most modern firms try very hard to avoid such changes. Delivery periods are more likely to lengthen. In the case of a large and persistent fall in demand there may be some 'weak' selling. But here also most modern firms try to hold their prices constant until demand recovers. These deviations from the pattern of adjustment predicted by the perfect competition model imply that the model is not appropriate for most modern industries.

3. The model predicts that all firms making the same product will be of the same – optimum – size. There is some tendency in this direction in parts of agriculture in some countries. But in modern industries and services all the evidence points towards a quite different conclusion. A difficulty in testing this prediction in such industries arises from the fact that there are very few, if any, industries in which each firm produces only one identical product. Lack of homogeneity of product, or product differentiation, is itself in conflict with the assumptions of the perfect competition model. Nevertheless, we may ask whether empirical evidence on the size of firms in particular 'industries' (usually defined either by the similarity of their products or by the similarity of their technologies) is consistent with the probability that, if there were many firms producing the same product, they would be of similar size. The statistics of firm sizes (more often of plant sizes) show enormous size differences in most industries, with a multitude of very small firms (employing less than 5 or 10 workers) and a tiny handful of giant firms employing 10,000 or more workers. There is scarcely ever any sign of a dominant central frequency, or 'mode', in such distributions; and this suggests that the concept of an 'optimum' size of firm in these industries is inconsistent with the facts. A similar conclusion follows from numerous studies of long-period cost curves and economies of scale.
4. According to the model of perfect competition, long-run adjustments in supply occur through changes in the number of optimum firms producing the given product, not by changes in

the scale of output of existing firms. This prediction, of course, follows from the prediction discussed immediately above. In a few industries, in which small firms predominate, there may be a tendency in this direction. The most obvious examples are in personal services, such as hairdressing. But over the great bulk of industry, including farming and building, which behave in some respects according to the model of perfect competition, empirical experience runs completely contrary to the prediction. Long-run adjustments in output are made predominantly by changes in the scale of output of existing firms.

5. If, as assumed in the model of perfect competition, technology were a free good, all existing firms and all potential new entrants would know precisely how to produce a given product with 'best practice' technique, at minimum cost for given factor prices, and without any 'X-inefficiency'. A mass of scattered evidence, largely of an anecdotal kind, suggests that this prediction deviates widely from the facts. In addition, two specific predictions which follow from the general prediction are clearly falsified by experience. These predictions are that there will never be an incentive for foreign direct investment, and that less developed countries will not make insistent demands for the creation of institutions to facilitate the 'transfer of technology'.
6. Under perfect competition there would be no long-term differences in regional unemployment rates. Indeed, there would be a very low figure of general unemployment.
7. There would also be no difficulty in raising capital at a constant market rate of interest by any firm desiring to become established or to expand. Capital, like other goods, would be in infinitely elastic supply to the individual borrower.
8. Finally, under perfect competition there would be no role for the entrepreneur. With perfect knowledge of technology, perfect mobility of factors, and perfect markets for both products and factors, he would have no function. Since there would be no risks to be taken, and no problems of discovering and implementing good systems of organization and management, the essential factor in the growth and technical improvement of modern economies would be missing. Under perfect competition, with all

technical progress assumed to be exogenous, few of the great advances in technology of the past two or three centuries would have occurred.

CONCLUSIONS

In modern industrialized economies only a very small proportion of total output (probably less than 20 per cent) is produced or sold under conditions approximating to perfect competition in product markets. The great bulk of goods and services is sold at prices fixed by their producers, prices which do not vary with conditions of market demand but which are adjusted at longer intervals under the influence of changes in input costs. The underlying factors causing such changes will be discussed in Chapter 4.

So far as the factors of production are concerned, the proportion that is sold under conditions of perfect competition is even smaller. The price of labour is largely controlled by legislation, collective agreements, and custom; and the price of hiring capital is heavily influenced by the policies of governments and central banks. While employers of labour can usually obtain extra workers at the market wage, borrowers of capital are limited by the quality of their reputation and the size of their available collateral.

The model of perfect competition is useful up to a point in analysing the short-run behaviour of those few industries in which the appropriate conditions approximately apply. For example, when the supply of tomatoes increases, their price tends to fall; when the demand for houses increases, the prices of houses (both old and new) tend to increase, as well as the cost of making repairs. But perfect competition prices do not always move smoothly towards their new long-run equilibrium levels. Under the influence of speculation and time lags in the adjustment of supply, prices often 'overshoot' and follow a cobweb pattern of adjustment, which may even take a few years to settle down. At a macroeconomic level the business cycle is largely the result of the inherent instability of perfect competition; and the decline in its importance in recent decades is a reflection of the decline in the importance of perfect competition.

Even in the industries whose products are sold under conditions approximating to perfect competition the sizes of firms vary widely; there is no unique optimum size of firm; and (in most cases) expansion of supply is brought about primarily by an increase in output from existing firms rather than by an increase in the number of optimum firms. These phenomena suggest that, even where conditions approximating to perfect competition exist in product markets, there are important imperfections in the markets for the factors of production and technology.

The fundamental defect in the model of perfect competition is its (inevitable) assumption of perfect knowledge. While it is reasonable to assume near-perfect knowledge of the qualities and prices of most primary products, much technological knowledge (at least under conditions of free enterprise) is the private property of the firms which have discovered it, and knowledge of the future (which is necessary for making rational decisions about investment) is inherently unknowable with certainty, especially when it includes knowledge of the probable reactions of competitors. The perfect knowledge assumption is not only unrealistic but has a malign effect on the theory of economic development. For perfect knowledge of technology and of the future eliminates the role of the entrepreneur, who has been the principal historical agent of change and development. Perfect competition can, with suitable additional assumptions, account for the stationary state. But it cannot provide a coherent explanation of technical progress as it has actually happened, nor of the accompanying rate of economic growth.

In Chapter 3 we shall consider the effects on the model of perfect competition of removing the assumptions of perfect knowledge of technology and of perfect competition in factor markets. The combination of perfect competition in product markets with imperfect knowledge of technology and of imperfect competition in factor markets will be described as 'semi-perfect' competition. In Chapter 4 we shall proceed to an examination of the additional effects of imperfect competition in product markets. A theoretical model will then be suggested to incorporate the effects of all these imperfections.

3 Semi-perfect Competition

I use the phrase 'semi-perfect competition' to describe a combination of (approximately) perfect competition in product markets with imperfect competition in the supply of technology and of the hired factors of production. The combination of these perfect and imperfect ingredients creates a 'hybrid' type of competition, which is more realistic than perfect competition and, for that reason, more instructive and more theoretically useful. This hybrid type of competition is also an essential theoretical stepping stone towards the construction of a realistic model of imperfect competition in the normal sense. I shall start by considering the effects of imperfect knowledge of technology, and then examine the effects of imperfect competition in factor markets. The final section of this chapter will be concerned with the equilibrium of an industry operating under conditions of semi-perfect competition.

IMPERFECT KNOWLEDGE OF TECHNOLOGY

According to the standard model of perfect competition all existing and potential firms in an industry (where an industry is defined as a group of one-product firms that supply a given product) are confronted by a long-run average cost curve such as *LAC* in Figure 3.1. This curve represents the minimum average cost of production of a given product at various scales of output, when the firm is using 'best practice' technique, and when it buys or hires its inputs at fixed market prices (supplied under perfectly competitive conditions in both product and factor markets). In so far as the 'entrepreneur' is himself providing labour or capital to the business, the standard market costs of these should be included in *LAC*. But there are no costs attributable to entrepreneurship as such, because under perfect competition, with perfect knowledge of technology and of the future, there is no entrepreneurial function to be rewarded. Under conditions

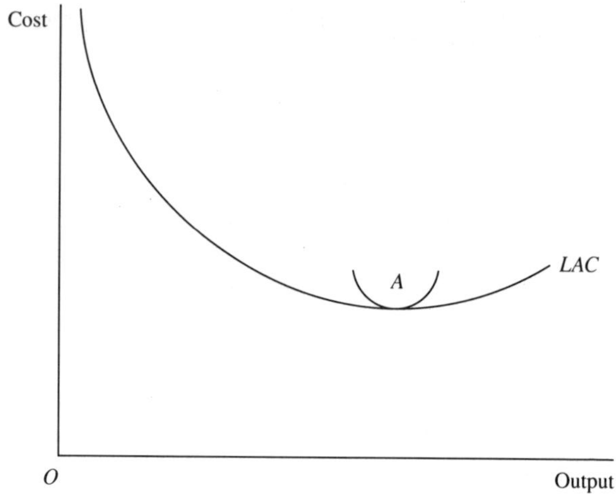

Figure 3.1

of 'free entry', therefore, there will be an infinitely elastic supply of 'entrepreneurs' to the industry at a zero price, and competition will ensure that in long-run equilibrium all firms in the industry will occupy the short-run average cost position *A*, which is tangential to the long-run average cost curve at its minimum point. This set of assumptions raises many questions, each of which will be considered in its proper place below. At this point we concentrate on the assumption about technology.

The assumption that the LAC curve is freely available to all potential new entrants implies that technical knowledge is a free good, perhaps a set of blueprints or instruction manuals obtainable free of charge. Since this is patently an absurd idea, we need to consider more precisely how technical knowledge is actually acquired.

Take the example of a man (or a woman) who is thinking of setting up as a farmer. In order to operate at a normal level of efficiency he needs to know at least the following: methods of cultivation of various crops and/or methods of rearing and caring for livestock; methods of maintaining and improving the quality of the land; methods of training and managing farm workers; methods of using, maintaining and repairing farm machinery; elementary accountancy; some clerical skills; methods of efficient buying and selling; and some knowledge of the law. Clearly, this wide range of knowledge is not available at zero cost. An intending farmer could obtain knowledge of some of these techniques from attendance at a farm school or college, and some from private study. But purely intellectual or armchair methods of study would not be sufficient to equip him to be an effective farmer. He would also need to have practical experience of farming methods, which could be obtained only by working on a farm, either as a family worker or as an employee. It is, I think, obvious that potential entrepreneurs in all other industries, who hope to be successful, have a similar need for practical experience.

This need for practical experience, or 'know-how', indicates that technical knowledge comes from two sources. While one type of knowledge of technology can be obtained from schools and other public institutions, from reading, from visiting exhibitions, from examining the products of existing producers, and so on, there is another type that can be obtained only by working in an existing enterprise. We can call the former type 'public' technology, and the latter type 'private' technology. Private technology includes all the special work practices of a particular firm, ranging from its engineering and other physical methods of processing materials, through the management of labour and capital, to buying, selling and many other business and administrative activities. It is important to understand that technology is not confined to engineering or other physical technology, as is often implied in the textbook treatment of the production function, but covers every aspect of business organization and decision-making. The *content* of technology can, therefore, be divided broadly into 'physical' and 'organizational' technology. Part of each of these two types of technology can be obtained from public sources, but an essential part is private. The private content is especially large in the case of organizational technology, since it is almost impossible to teach efficient systems of organization by purely verbal, and hence abstract, methods.[1]

Both physical and organizational technologies have a size dimension. The knowledge of how to operate efficiently, and maintain, a garden mower is more limited than the knowledge of how to operate efficiently, and maintain, a combine harvester. But the influence of size is much more important in the case of organizational technology. Many people can manage efficiently a one-man or family enterprise; very few can manage efficiently a firm employing 50–100 workers; and fewer still can manage efficiently a firm that employs many thousands of workers. The knowledge of how to manage efficiently large quantities of resources (physical, financial, and human) is learnt almost entirely by practical experience. While some people have an exceptional talent for large-scale organization (one thinks, for example, of an Alexander, a Napoleon, or a Henry Ford), no one can jump immediately, and without any previous organizational experience, into a position of authority in a large enterprise, and succeed.

If organizational technology is largely part of private technology, which must be acquired mainly by practical experience and, in particular, if the technology of managing large-scale organizations can be acquired only by previous experience of managing somewhat smaller organizations, it follows that, if the optimum size of firm in an industry is larger than a very small size, freedom of entry in itself does not guarantee that new entrants will be able immediately to establish themselves at an optimum size. In other words, in the absence of perfect knowledge of technology, the *LAC* curve in Figure 3.1 is not freely available to all potential new entrants; and actual new entrants will not automatically locate themselves at position *A*. Indeed, in the absence of perfect knowledge of technology, one can no longer assume that there is a unique *LAC* curve applicable to all firms. Each firm, or potential firm, will have it own *ex ante* estimates of costs at various points on its own *LAC* curve and, since private technologies differ, there is no reason to expect that such estimates will be the same for all firms. Since, in addition, *ex post* costs will differ from their *ex ante* estimates, the average relation between the measured average costs of firms in an industry and their outputs cannot be assumed to represent a true, or objective, *ex ante* relationship. Furthermore, in the absence of perfect knowledge of technology, there will be no unique optimum size of firm for each industry. Each firm's initial *ex ante* estimates are likely to suggest a different optimum size of firm; and, as time passes and the firm acquires additional private technology from its practical experience, its estimate of the optimum size may change.

The conclusion from this discussion is that most new entrants to a semi-perfectly competitive industry will be one-man or family firms. While it is possible that firms which have already acquired the organizational technology for efficient operation on a larger scale in one industry may decide to 'cross over' into another industry, this is an unlikely event under semi-perfectly competitive conditions, when most firms will be of small or medium size. In actual experience 'cross overs' occur mostly under conditions of imperfect competition in product markets, when products are differentiated and most firms are multi-product. The effects of 'cross overs' will, therefore, be considered further in Chapter 4.

IMPERFECT FACTOR MARKETS

If the factors of production were in perfectly elastic supply to all firms, new entrants that had successfully established themselves on the smallest scale, and that had gradually acquired experience of the physical and organizational technology necessary for successful operation on a somewhat larger scale would be able to hire additional labour and capital at standard market rates and, combining these additional factors with their newly acquired knowledge, would be able to operate successfully on that larger scale. (By 'successfully' in this context we mean having average costs corresponding to those depicted in their own 'best practice' *LAC* curve.) But actual factor markets are not, and never have been, perfectly competitive, even for firms operating under conditions of perfect competition in their product markets.

In the case of capital, the firm's demand is normally for liquid capital, i.e. for cash which can be used for investment in machinery, materials, credits to customers and so forth. The borrowing firm incurs a responsibility to return the loan, also in cash, at some future date or dates; but in the meantime it usually has complete freedom in determining the uses of the loan. In these circumstances, the lender has little guarantee that the physical or financial assets for which the loan is used will be realizable, if needed, in order to finance the repayment of the loan. The lender's uncertainty about the security of his loan from this source is further increased by the influence of 'moral hazard', i.e. by his uncertainty about the borrower's honesty or reliability in carrying out his stated intentions. As a result, no firm can normally obtain external finance without, first, having previously established a good reputation for efficient operation and honest performance of contracts and, second, being able to offer suitable collateral. Formally speaking, collateral means the earmarking of specific assets already owned by the firm, which it is obliged to surrender to the borrower in the event of default. But, in a broader sense, collateral includes the existence of substantial owner's equity in the enterprise, which provides a cushion for creditors in the case of financial difficulties. In general, therefore, firms are limited in the amount of their borrowing by the size of their existing equity, according to some rough rule of maximum gearing. Moreover, since borrowing increases the owner's risk, he himself is often reluctant to borrow up to the maximum gearing ratio which lenders would accept.

It follows from this inevitable element of imperfection in the capital market that new entrants to a semi-perfectly competitive industry will not be able to expand solely on the basis of having acquired the technological experience for operating successfully on a larger scale. They will also have to overcome the difficulty of obtaining the necessary additional capital from an imperfect capital market. Many new entrants will try to rely entirely on their own ploughed back profits for this purpose. Those which have greater confidence in their own abilities may also be willing to incur the risk of borrowing. But even these will be limited by the maximum gearing ratio imposed by the lenders. In all cases, therefore, a prerequisite for expansion will be some addition to owner's equity, normally from ploughed back profits. When these conditions are satisfied, a successful new entrant will be able to move gradually down his *LAC* curve in the direction of the optimum scale (if such exists).

Important imperfections also exist in the labour market. Even if the institutional imperfections imposed by trade unions and labour legislation are left on one side, there remains another intrinsic labour market imperfection, especially in a modern industrialized economy. This is illustrated by the fact that no firm can normally expect to obtain as many additional workers *of the desired type* as it wishes at the standard market wage. The reason is that, under modern conditions, workers are highly differentiated. And this differentiation is not so much by 'public' skills, i.e. skills which can be acquired outside enterprises, but mainly by 'private' skills. Private skills, like private technology, are created within enterprises: they encompass the specific methods, both physical and organizational, with which the enterprise operates. Indeed, private skills and private technology are two sides of the same coin. Private skills, like private technology, can be learnt only by practical experience, by 'on-the-job training.' Consequently, an employer who is looking for extra workers has to consider not only their public skills but also their likely abilities to acquire his private skills, and to fit into his existing team. Selection and training of new workers take time – often a great deal of time, especially for workers who carry greater responsibilities. As a result, it is not normally possible for a firm to expand its scale of operations rapidly without a reduction in its efficiency. This factor, like the need to accumulate extra internal capital, acts as a brake on the speed of growth of firms towards their preferred size.[2]

There are, of course, other obstacles to the rapid expansion of a firm, even under perfectly competitive conditions in its product market. These include the need to find suitable land in a suitable location. If expansion involves an increase in the size of existing plant, there may be great, or even insuperable, difficulties in finding suitable land. This is why plants established on 'greenfield' sites are often much more efficient than those which have grown from smaller beginnings on old sites. But only a firm with sound experience in organizing large plants can normally take the risk of starting on a greenfield site. This is one respect in which foreign firms have a considerable advantage over their domestic rivals.

EQUILIBRIUM OF THE INDUSTRY

It has been suggested above that under conditions of semi-perfect competition each firm – and each potential new entrant – has its own *ex ante LAC* curve. These curves may be U-shaped, reverse J-shaped, or L-shaped; but most firms, and especially potential new entrants, will have no definite opinion about which of these shapes is correct. What they will believe is that, at least over some range starting from the point of entry, there are likely to be significant economies of scale. Hence, new entrants will usually look forward to the possibility of expanding their businesses over that range. Some more enterprising and imaginative new entrants may even look further forward and picture themselves as medium or large-scale firms which can earn large profits. But the exact shape of the *LAC* curve under conditions of semi-perfect competition is largely irrelevant to the decisions of new entrants, and to the equilibrium price level at which the product is sold. It remains true, of course, that at some point in a firm's expansion its directors may come to the conclusion that there would be no great advantage in further growth, in other words, that the firm has reached the point of minimum long-run average cost, or has even gone beyond it. But this cannot be foreseen with accuracy at an earlier stage, because in the earlier stages of its growth a firm cannot predict what level of private technology it will attain later.

Irrespective of the ultimate shape of their *LAC* curves, new entrants to an industry operating under conditions of semi-perfect competition will be almost entirely one-man or family firms. Some of these entrepreneurs will be more efficient than others, some will have more drive and ambition, and some will have better luck. The more efficient, the more hard-working, and the more fortunate will have lower costs per unit than the others, and hence higher incomes, out of which, if they wish, they will be able to save more and plough back more saving into their businesses. In general, it will be these kinds of firm which will start to pull away from the others, in terms of size, and hence in terms of costs and profits. The less successful new entrants will either exist in a state of long-term stagnation or eventually abandon the industry. Experience shows that very large numbers of new firms die every year. This is, indeed, a process of 'natural selection'.

Whether the more profitable new entrants will expand depends on the entrepreneurial spirit of their owners. In general, we can assume that most of them would not have entered the industry in he first place unless they had had the ambition (and accompanying determination) to expand. As these firms expand, they will accumulate more private technology and more equity capital; and these will ease the way for further expansion. But, since even the best enterprise is always at the mercy of unexpected events, some of these early succeeders will fall by the wayside at a later stage. Those which continue to expand will be continually mastering new private technology, both physical and organizational. At first, this technology will be a monopoly of the firm which creates it. But there is a constant tendency for private technology to seep out into the public domain. Patents expire; workers and managers move from one firm to another and carry knowledge of private technology with them; and eventually all firms have to expose aspects of their methods to public scrutiny, by putting their products on the market, or by inviting customers to visit their premises. As private technology is converted into public technology, the originating firms lose part of their monopoly of knowledge, and the whole industry is able to improve its performance. This is an example, in the field of technology, of Adam Smith's 'invisible hand', which converts private gain into a public benefit. In terms of the *LAC* curves, this means that as individual firms move down their individual curves of *ex post* experience they tend to pull down the levels of the *ex ante* curves of their competitors.

A snapshot of the distribution of firms in such an industry after a number of years might be expected to look like Figure 3.2. The points in this diagram are intended to represent average actual cost per unit of each firm, measured against its actual output in a given period. These points will not usually be at the minimum of the firm's short-run average cost curve, since for almost all firms price will exceed minimum average cost and output will be to the right of that point. While, for reasons already discussed, there is no unique industry-wide *LAC* curve, the observed group of surviving firms can be thought of as being arranged around a downward-sloping curve of average experience. If there is a steady stream of hopeful new entrants, the population of surviving firms will be heavily concentrated at the lowest levels of output, and it will thin out rapidly at higher levels (with a distribution similar to that of runners in a marathon race after the race has been in progress for some time, and on the assumption that the laggards drop out or are excluded). Although there are considerable difficulties in finding appropriate data for firms that produce homogeneous products, all available size distributions of firms or plants in industries that approximate to such conditions are of this highly skew type. Not one, to my knowledge, shows the pattern that would prevail if the model of perfect competition were correct, namely a clustering of firms or plants around a single point. Moreover, from an inspection of scatter diagrams it is usually not easy to determine whether average *ex post* costs begin to rise at some point. There may be one large firm, like *F* in Figure 3.2, which has higher average costs than firms of somewhat smaller size; but there may be also a large firm like *G* which has lower costs.

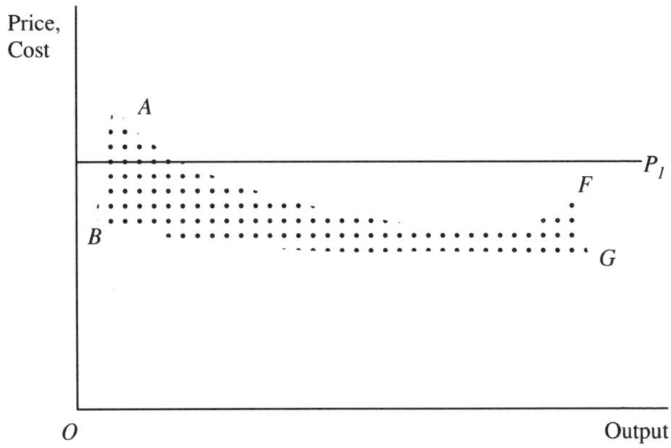

Figure 3.2

A snapshot diagram like Figure 3.2 tells us that all firms are in a condition which would be described, under perfect competition assumptions, as long-run disequilibrium. In what sense, then, can we say that this is really a picture of an equilibrium? The answer is that the observed distribution of firms is the result of a balance between various forces, some of which encourage the expansion of the firm while others hold it back. The outcome of this balance of forces is that, at any particular moment of time, there will be a particular size distribution of firms of different sizes and levels of cost, and hence a particular total output from the industry and a particular total of cost and – when we know the market price for the product – a particular total value of output and total amount of profit.

How is the equilibrium price of the product determined? The price, under these semi-perfect competitive conditions, is represented in the diagram by a horizontal straight line. When that price is higher, each firm already in existence will produce more in the short run, and in the long run the higher price will attract more new entrants, permit more of them to survive, and provide higher profits to the larger firms, on the basis of which they will tend to expand the scale of their activities more rapidly. As in the standard model of perfect competition, therefore, a higher price will promote a larger output, both in the short run and in the long run. In the opposite case, a lower price will discourage new entry, cut short the life of many existing small firms, and reduce the profits of larger firms; all of which will tend to reduce output in the short run and to slow down its expansion in the long run. When there is a constant level of demand, the short-run equilibrium price will be that which leads to a total output from surviving firms equal to that total demand. This price is represented in Figure 3.2. by the line P_1.

At the price P_1 most firms will be making profits, but it is very probable that some, especially of the smaller firms, will be making losses. A firm like *A*, for example, has average costs in excess of the market price. Nevertheless, it may decide to continue to operate, at least for some time, if the owner is prepared to accept a lower remuneration for his own labour and capital than he could expect to receive in the open market. He will be encouraged to do this, first, if it would be difficult in practice to transfer his labour and capital from its present employment and obtain the standard market rates of remuneration for them; second, if he gains non-financial benefits from being his own master; and third, if he is still hopeful that his luck will change. There is much evidence that, at any moment of time, there are many small firms that do not cover their opportunity costs of labour and capital. Clearly, if the price were lower than P_1, a firm like *B* might also find itself making losses, while firms like *A* would be under increasing pressure to close down.

It should be noted that, in this model, there is no position of short-run equilibrium that is consistent with long-run equilibrium in the traditional sense. For example, at the price P_1 which yields short-run equilibrium, most surviving firms will be making profits, and will have both the incentive and the means to expand the scale of their operations in the long run. So long as some surviving firms are making profits there will be a continued upward creep of long-run supply. In the limit, the expansion of long-run supply may be checked only by establishing a short-run equilibrium price so low as to concentrate all production in the hands of a few large firms. At this point, semi-perfect competition would cease to exist, and be replaced by oligopoly. Consequently, under conditions of semi-perfect competition the equilibrium which is established after some firms have entered or left the industry cannot be described as a 'long-run' equilibrium, as conventionally defined. For, even after the adjustment in the number of firms, new investment will continue as some firms continue to expand. We shall, therefore, describe this form of equilibrium as 'structural' equilibrium. Unlike the long-run equilibrium of perfect competition, which is static, the structural equilibrium of semi-perfect competition is dynamic.

DIFFERENCES BETWEEN THE PREDICTIONS OF PERFECT AND SEMI-PERFECT COMPETITION

We may conclude this chapter by summarizing the main differences in the predictions of the models of perfect and semi-perfect competition. First, as regards the size distribution of firms, the former model predicts that all firms in an industry will be approximately of the same size and will have similar unit costs; the latter model predicts that the size distribution of firms will be highly skew, and that, on the average, the unit costs of medium and larger firms will be lower than those of small firms.

Secondly, when demand for the industry's product changes, the former model predicts that long-run adjustment will be achieved, not by a change in the sizes of existing firms, but by an increase or decrease in the number of firms of optimum size. The latter model, on the other hand, predicts that an increase in demand will be satisfied, after full structural adjustment, by *both* an increase in the number of firms in the industry (predominantly small new entrants) *and* an increase in the size of existing firms; while, in the case of a fall in demand, the long-run adjustment will consist of a decline in the number of small firms and a slowing down in the rate of growth of larger firms.

Thirdly, while the model of perfect competition predicts that, in long-run equilibrium, all firms will have zero profits, the model of semi-perfect competition predicts that in structural equilibrium the distribution of profits will be widely dispersed and positively related to the size of firm.

Fourthly, following from the previous prediction, the model of perfect competition predicts that, when the price of the product falls, all firms will make losses (and presumably all will have an equal incentive to close down), while the model of semi-perfect competition predicts that, in similar circumstances, only some firms (and predominantly the smaller ones) will make losses while many will continue to make profits.

Fifthly, the model of perfect competition predicts that a condition of long-run equilibrium will be static, and will only change as a result of changes in exogenous factors. In particular, technical progress comes only from outside the firm, 'like manna from heaven'. The model of semi-perfect competition, on the other hand, predicts that a condition of structural equilibrium is 'dynamic', in the sense that changes in technology and scale are endogenous to the given structure of firms. The initiator and instrument of these changes is the entrepreneur, who is crucial to the explanation of the model of semi-perfect competition, but who has no function under conditions of perfect competition, and strictly speaking should not even be mentioned in that model.

4 Fixprice Competition

Under conditions of either perfect or semi-perfect competition goods and services are, in effect, sold at auction to the highest bidder. Services have scarcely ever been sold like that; and, even in medieval times, most artisan products were sold in a different fashion. In modern industrialized economies only a very small proportion of total output – at most about 10–20 per cent – is sold by auction. The great bulk of products is sold at prices fixed by their producers or sellers. I have borrowed from Professor Hicks the term 'fixprice' to describe this type of market.

There are probably three main reasons for the rise of fixprice competition. The first is the growth in the importance of manufactures and services in comparison with primary products. Although man has played a major role in the development of new kinds of farm products, it is only rarely that a single producer has been able to retain a monopoly of such new varieties, even for a short period; and mineral products are almost entirely 'given' by nature. But as soon as men start fabricating manufactured products they have scope for the introduction of their own designs. The same opportunities have always existed in the supply of services.

The second probable reason has been growing discontent with the inherent instability of perfectly competitive markets. Under conditions of perfect or semi-perfect competition prices are constantly changing, mainly as a result of changes in supply. The supply of farm products can rise or fall by many percentage points because of changes in the weather; and the supply of simple manufactures (such as cotton textiles in the nineteenth century) can vary widely as a consequence of changes in the numbers of producers and of their scales of output. Moreover, the resulting fluctuations in prices often have seriously disturbing long-term effects, with many new firms entering or leaving markets in response to current and expected changes in prices, thus causing problems of 'overshoot'. One of the functions of entrepreneurs is to bear the burden of uncertainty. But it is natural that they should try to reduce the level and character of uncertainty as much as possible. Price uncertainty is one of the worst forms of uncertainty because, under competitive conditions, there is nothing that the entrepreneur can do about it. He is at the mercy of the uncontrollable forces of the market. If he can exclude this dimension of uncertainty, he can concentrate his efforts (and his anxieties) on areas in which he can make some impression, in particular on improving productivity and increasing his share of the market.

A third possible reason is that firms operating in a perfectly competitive market come to recognize that, if the only way in which they can raise their long-term profitability is through improvements in productivity, such improvements will increase aggregate supply and hence reduce the market price. So, from their own point of view, part of their effort is wasted. If, instead, they can concentrate on increasing their *share* of the market, there will be no automatic tendency for the price to fall, and the full benefit of the increase in their sales (after subtracting the cost of bringing that about) will accrue to them alone.

None of these motives for moving towards fixprice competition is associated with a desire to exploit the consumer by establishing a monopoly. The role of private monopolies has been greatly exaggerated in economic theory. The most dangerous monopolies are those established by governments, under laws that prescribe that the production or sale of a particular product is reserved exclusively for a privileged supplier. Private monopolies, in the strict sense, are rare, and usually only transitory so long as there are no statutory prohibitions on the entry of potential competitors. The use of the term 'monopolistic competition' to describe fixprice competition has, in my opinion, introduced an undesirable bias both in attitudes and in the method of analysis of the condition.

THE FIXING OF THE PRICE

The key to removing the price instability of perfect competition is product differentiation. Once the producer or seller has established that he has a different product, he can fix its price and concentrate his efforts on increasing its output or sale. At what level will he fix the price? Before we address that question directly it is necessary to consider the implications of product differentiation for the concept of the firm and for its incentive to grow.

In both the previous chapters we followed the standard textbook assumption that a firm is a business that produces a single product. That is the only basis on which one can draw a diagram of a firm's marginal and average costs against its physical output, measured in terms of a single product. That is also the basis for the usual justification for the assumed shapes of the various cost curves. In effect, the firm is assumed to consist of a single plant. While this assumption is obviously incorrect in many cases, it is probably sufficiently close to reality when we are considering conditions of semi-perfect competition. (Whether it is close to reality under conditions of perfect competition is irrelevant, since perfect competition as a whole is, for reasons given above, an unrealistic model.) But as soon as we move to fixprice competition, which arises out of product differentiation, it is clear that we can no longer proceed on the assumption that each firm produces only one product. In fact, as casual observation demonstrates, under modern conditions the one-product firm hardly exists at all in manufacturing, construction or services, and is quite rare in agriculture. The only industries in which it is predominant are mining and plantations. When firms are multi-product, two important questions arise. The first is: what is now meant by 'the firm'? The second is: how does the existence of many products affect the cost curves for the individual products?

In earlier chapters we have implicitly assumed, as is conventionally the rule, that we know what is meant by 'the firm'. This is perhaps a reasonable assumption in a world of one-product firms. For 'the firm' is then an organization which produces a single product with a view to making maximum profits. But in our discussion of semi-perfect competition we have drawn attention to the importance of private technology, which is a collection of physical and organizational 'know-how' possessed by a particular firm. A firm is normally a continuing 'living organism', with its own history, structure, methods of working, and traditions, which constitute its private technology. Indeed, I think that we can go further and state that *a firm is a business organization defined by its private technology*. The assets of every firm are, of course, owned by someone and, so long as all, or most, of the assets are owned by one person or group, it might be argued that that person or group identifies the firm. But assets can be sold; yet the firm continues. What continues, I suggest, is the stock of private technology. At any moment of time, this stock of private technology is held by a particular group of owners, managers, and other employees. But, when the composition of that group changes, the stock of private technology remains. (A similar analysis can be applied to almost any human institution, such as an army, a church, a school, a legal or political system, or a nation. All have their changing stocks of 'private technology'.)

Is there any reason to believe that the shapes of the cost curves for individual products in a multi-product firm follow the pattern of cost curves of the product of a one-product firm? An immediate difficulty appears, in that the cost of producing a single product in a multi-product firm cannot be determined with precision, since overhead (or indirect) costs have to be attributed to each product, and this is ultimately an arbitrary process. Nevertheless, since the economies of large-scale production still apply to each product separately, average direct costs for each product can be assumed to be falling over some range, and perhaps indefinitely. As regards indirect costs, we may assume that most firms would not add a new product to their range of products unless they thought that the additional indirect costs would not exceed the margin of price over direct costs of the new product, in other words that the introduction of the new product would add to total profits.

We may, I think, go further than this. Since we shall assume 'free entry', every firm which adds a new product to its range needs to take into account the possibility that a similar product could be marketed by a one-product firm. This means that the multi-product firm cannot allow its total costs per unit for any single product to depart too far from the costs of producing a similar product in a one-product firm. In general, therefore, a multi-product firm will have an incentive to increase its size at least as great as the incentives of firms producing each of its products on a one-product basis. This implies that many, or most, multi-product firms will tend to grow over time on the basis of their accumulated private technology and ploughed back profits, just as most one-product firms grow under semi-perfect competition.

We can now return to the original question: how are prices fixed by fixprice firms? In the standard textbook treatment of imperfect or monopolistic competition it is assumed that a (one-product) firm which has a differentiated product, and therefore its own separate demand curve, will aim to maximize its profit, like a monopolist, by choosing the price at which marginal revenue is equal to marginal cost. Having taken this decision, the firm then discovers that its abnormal profits attract the entry of new firms, which proceed to offer products closely similar to its own, and possibly at a lower price. The original firm loses customers; its demand curve is shifted to the left; and this process continues until all abnormal profits have been squeezed out. The firm's demand curve is then tangential to its long-run average cost curve at a point to the left of the minimum of the latter curve. We are left with higher prices and higher costs than under perfect competition, and with excess capacity.

This standard story seems at first sight to be an impressive piece of analysis, with interesting practical implications. But it requires only a few moments of reflection to realize that it is totally contrary to common sense. We start with individual firms that have taken the trouble to differentiate their products (for one or more of the reasons given above), and that have thus acquired a valuable property – 'their own' market. The textbooks then assume that such a firm will think only about its *immediate* profit-maximizing opportunities, and fix its price at a level that will attract competitors. If it follows such a policy, not only will it lose the possibility of making 'abnormal' profits but, since the competitors attracted into the market may well take away a considerable part of its market share, it may find itself making losses. Above all, the degree of certainty about its own market, and the price of its product, that it had hoped to achieve by product differentiation will have been lost. The policy assumed in the textbooks is myopic and irrational, and could make sense only to people who believed that they lived in a static world. While some economists may have persuaded themselves that the world is like that, it is impossible to believe that businessmen take that view.

The only rational policy for a firm that has a differentiated product is to fix its price at a point that is expected to yield maximum profits *in the long run*. That means that short-term profits must be weighed against longer term losses, and other sources of discomfort. Most firms with any significant investment in their business will prefer to take longer views, and try to protect their market share. They will resist the temptation to maximize immediate profits, and will fix their prices predominantly by considering the level at which the entry of new competitors into their market is discouraged. This policy, sometimes described as 'limit pricing', has been discussed in connection with the analysis of oligopoly, and has been suggested as one *possible* response of oligopoly firms to the threat of new entry.[1]

But it has a much wider application. Limit pricing, or 'entry deterring' pricing, is the logical policy for all firms which have differentiated products or markets. It is a general policy appropriate to 'small groups', 'large groups', and even to the case of private monopoly, so long as there is any risk of new entry.

While there can be no doubt that a rational firm with a differentiated product will fix its price only after taking into account the probable repercussions of that price on the decisions of new entrants, it is not possible to define on *a priori* grounds precisely how much weight the rational firm will give to the various elements of these repercussions. We are in a world where expectations are important, perhaps decisive, in determining current policy, and there is no neat model of the static equilibrium type which can pretend to tell us what the outcome will be. Each firm will have different estimates of future events, will give them different probabilities, and will give them different weights in influencing its decisions. But we can identify some considerations which are likely to be relevant. (In this chapter we shall limit ourselves to the case of a closed economy. The additional problems that arise in an open economy will considered in Chapter 8.)

First, we need to clarify what is meant in this context by 'new entry'. We are no longer in a world of perfect or semi-perfect competition. Each firm has its own differentiated product, or products. Strictly speaking there can be, in this world, no such thing as 'new entry', since there is no industry producing a homogeneous product which can be 'entered'. The entry threat to a firm making a differentiated product is the threat that another firm will start to produce or sell a product closely similar to its own, either in its technical specifications or in its appearance, packaging, or advertising. Since we are now in a world where most firms produce many different products, new entry does not require the creation of a new firm. All that may happen is that an existing firm will diversify its product range. This is what we earlier called a 'cross over'.

Secondly, as we have argued above, multi-product fixprice firms, like one-product firms in conditions of semi-perfect competition, will have different levels of average cost for their products, depending on the volume of output of the given product. On the average, larger firms – at least up to some size – will have lower average costs or, to put the same point slightly differently, will have, for any given level of price, a larger margin of profit per unit over cost. Firms which are already in existence, and which have usually grown over the years to their present size, will know that, on the average, they can expect to obtain somewhat higher margins than they obtained when they were smaller. This will give them some guide to the margin which they can safely charge to prevent new entry.

But, thirdly, the 'safe margin' is not a definite amount which can be looked up in a book of tables. It remains the firm's own estimate of what it can safely get away with. This estimate can be based in part on the firm's own past experience, and perhaps on information obtained through the trade about the margins charged by other firms in a similar line of business. Ultimately, however, the test of the margin is whether it actually leads to new entrants or not. Firms which try to exploit their 'monopoly' position too much will suffer the consequences. By a process of 'natural selection' the firms that survive will be those which made the best estimates of a safe margin. In this manner, a structure of safe margins may be established.

In practice, the costs that form the base on which firms calculate their margins do not include the costs of overhead and capital. Instead, the firm estimates the direct labour and material costs of each item and adds a margin to cover overhead and 'profit', where 'profit' includes the implicit cost of capital. The most obvious reason for this procedure is that, since virtually all firms are multi-product, and since the science of cost accounting has not yet found an infallible method of allocating indirect costs to each product, the best 'rule of thumb' is to add a margin to cover these costs to the costs which can unambiguously be attributed to the product.

Behind this, however, there may lie a deeper influence on the structure of margins. When the costs of overhead and capital are excluded, the shape of the average relation between costs and scale of output, such as that suggested in Figure 3.2, may be somewhat different. The cost of capital per unit of output will often be higher for small firms than for those of medium or larger size (because of indivisibilities and a higher risk element), but the cost of overhead will usually be lower. In spite of any modifications made to the shape of the curve on this account, it seems probable that very small firms earn, on the average, very little surplus over direct costs, the labour element of which usually consists almost exclusively of the earnings of the owner and members of his family. If this is so, the market-established margin over direct costs for the very small firm will be approximately zero, and the margins that larger firms can safely charge are, in comparison with this, a 'surplus', or rent of their superior technical knowledge and ability to obtain capital. If the ultimate anchor of the system of margins is this approximately zero margin of the very small firm, the absolute level of each margin is determined.

THE EQUILIBRIUM OF THE FIRM

Let us now assume that a firm selling a differentiated product has made an estimate of its safe margin over direct costs for that product, and has accordingly fixed its selling price. What will be its short-run equilibrium position? Figure 4.1 illustrates its situation. *OR* is the fixed price, *MC* is the firm's short-run marginal cost curve and *DD* is its demand curve. In practice, the firm will not know much about its demand curve, apart from point *A*, which is given by its current sales. Since the firm has already decided that any price above *OR* would be unwise, the section of the demand curve above the line *RS* is irrelevant. The section of the demand curve below *RS* might be relevant if the firm thought that the demand curve in that

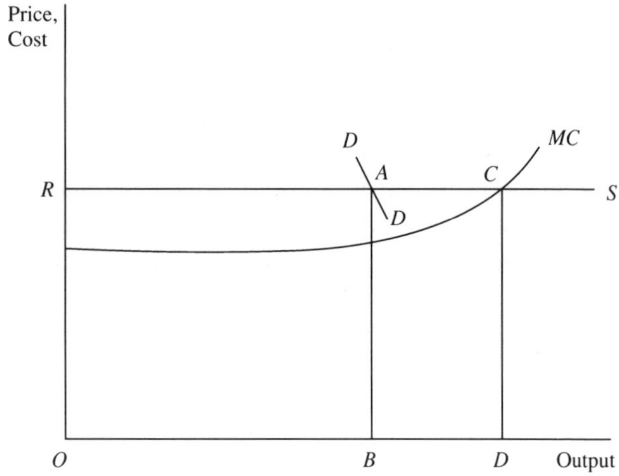

Figure 4.1

area was sufficiently elastic to make it worth its while to reduce its price below *OR*. But, first, the firm has little means of knowing whether this is so or not. Secondly experiments with reducing price often turn out to be very costly, either directly in terms of loss of profits or through inciting rival firms to cut their prices in retaliation. In the absence of empirical evidence about the elasticity of its demand curve, therefore, the firm will be likely to rely on general reasoning. If, for example, its margin of price over marginal cost is not more than 20 per cent of the price, the elasticity of demand below the price *OR* would need to be more than 5 to justify a price cut. In other words, a price cut of 5 per cent would be justified if the firm could be reasonably sure of increasing its sales by at least 25 per cent. This would be, for most firms, a very optimistic expectation; and, in view of the risks of such a policy, they will usually prefer to maintain the price *OR* and devote their energies rather to trying to increase their share of the market at that price.

At the fixed price *OR* the firm's sales will fluctuate with the state of demand in general, and with its 'share' of the market. (Since all products are differentiated, the word 'share' is not strictly accurate, but it is widely used by businesses to indicate their degree of success in comparison with their nearby rivals.) In the normal case, a firm will not be prepared to supply more than the quantity *OD* at the given price, because at outputs beyond this its marginal cost is in excess of the price. The point *C*, therefore, may be regarded as indicating the point of 'full capacity' operation in the short run. As sales approach this point, the firm will usually try to increase its capacity. But that, of course, will take time; and, for that reason, firms will usually aim always to keep a certain margin of excess capacity, and to take decisions on expansion of capacity early enough to avoid finding that the demand for their product has moved beyond their output capacity at the given price. In exceptional cases, firms which find themselves in that position may decide temporarily to produce beyond their 'capacity', i.e. at a loss on the extra sales, in order to avoid losing customers to rivals. Many firms seem to try to get over this temporary problem by accumulating unfilled orders. But only a few firms will be tempted to depart from their normal long-term policy and raise their price above *OR*. If they do succumb to that temptation, they will usually live to regret it.

For the reasons given in Chapter 3, almost all firms will have an incentive to expand their scale of operations. Consequently, they will constantly be trying to shift their demand curves to the right by improving the design or presentation of their products, or by advertising; or they will try to improve their physical or organization methods so as to reduce their costs. Very often, these two go hand in hand, since better production methods can more easily be introduced when output is expanding than when it is stagnant or falling.

SOME IMPLICATIONS OF THE MODEL

The above model can be applied, as already mentioned, to all firms which produce or sell differentiated products, whether they form part of a 'small group' or of a 'large group'. It can even be applied to a firm that is a 'monopoly', provided that there are no legal or institutional impediments to the entry of competing firms, i.e. provided that the monopoly always has to look over its shoulder for the threat of new entry. New entry, it should be recalled, does not usually mean the establishment of a completely new firm but rather the introduction of a closely competitive product by an existing firm. This model can, therefore, be regarded as a *general* model appropriate to all cases of differentiated products, i.e. to at least 80 per cent of output in modern industrialized economies. There are some interesting implications of the model to which special attention should be drawn.

First, this model provides a simple explanation for a number of other theories of the firm. The 'kinked demand curve' model is one attempt to account for the behaviour of a fixprice firm that is located at a point like *A*. But this model relies on the existence of two demand curves for the firm's product, one of which is applicable if the price of the product is raised and the other if the price of the product is reduced. The reason given for these two types of consumer response is that in the former case rival firms will keep their prices constant, while in the latter case they will reduce their prices in line with the firm which has cut its price. The explanation given for this asymmetrical response is that, once a firm has fixed its price, and hence its share of the market, rival firms will gladly allow the firm to lose some of that share, but will stoutly resist any attempt to increase it. But the model does not provide an explanation for the firm's initial price and market share; and this is a fatal weakness. In our model, on the other hand, there is a clear solution to this problem. The same applies to the 'theory' that firms aim to maximize their sales, since in the fixprice model, once a firm has fixed its price on the basis of its estimates of the threat of new entry, it can safely give most of its attention to the expansion of its sales at that price.

Secondly, the fixprice model provides a simple explanation of the fact that businessmen do not try to make marginal cost equal to marginal revenue. For reasons given above, almost all firms will take it for granted that their marginal revenue from a particular product is equal to the product's previously fixed price. And, so long as any firm is producing a particular product below capacity, it will know that the marginal cost of that product is below its price. The idea of equalizing marginal revenue and marginal price is, in these circumstances, absurd.

Thirdly, the model provides a simple explanation for the tendency of firms to adjust their prices in the same proportion as any change in their direct costs per unit. On this basis, the common notions of 'cost plus', and 'cost-induced inflation' can readily be understood.

Fourthly, the model provides a clear interpretation of the 'accelerator' principle. As a firm's sales increase, the point A moves towards the point C; i.e. the firm's output approaches its capacity. The closer that point A is to point C the more likely it is that the firm will take a decision to increase its capacity; and this normally means that it will order new investment. Similarly, when the point A moves to the left, the gap between output and capacity increases, and the immediate motive for making investment decisions is reduced. (Sophisticated firms may, however, consider that the best time to expand capacity is precisely when output is well below capacity, when investment costs are likely to be lower than at the peak of a boom).

Fifthly, the model provides a rational basis for the assumption in Keynesian theory that, over a certain range, an increase in demand may be accommodated without a significant increase in prices. But this assumption is valid only so long as the increased demand does not raise the prices of primary products, imports, and labour, the costs of which are automatically passed on proportionately in the final prices of fixprice firms.

In conclusion, it must be remembered that the whole of the above discussion has been concerned with a closed economy. In an open economy firms have to make decisions about prices in export markets as well as in domestic markets; and this creates some different problems. This topic will be taken up in Chapter 8, which is concerned with a number of wider issues.

In both this chapter and the previous one, i.e. under both fixprice and semi-perfect competition, we have seen that the accumulation of private technology and internal capital enables firms to grow, and thus to take advantage of the opportunities of increasing their profits. But this mechanism will operate only if the firm is controlled by an active entrepreneur. The entire system of technical progress and growth, not only for the individual firm but for the economy as a whole, depends on the activities of entrepreneurs. The models of competition that we have offered in place of perfect competition may, therefore, be conveniently described as models of 'entrepreneurial' competition. Because of the crucial role played by entrepreneurs in both the process of competition and the improvement in technology, two subsequent chapters will be devoted to them. In the first of these (Chapter 6) we shall consider the precise role of the entrepreneur, and in the second (Chapter 7) we shall consider the factors influencing the supply of entrepreneurs. But first we must discuss the optimality of entrepreneurial forms of competition, and compare it with the optimality of perfect competition.

5 Optimality

Theoretical work on the optimality of perfect competition has been so extensive that, despite the well-known deviations of perfect competition from optimality, there is a strong predisposition among economists to assume that any move away from perfect competition is a move away from an ideal state. Our suggestion that the only kinds of competition that can exist in practice are semi-perfect or fixprice competition will be likely, therefore, to attract the immediate criticism that such models imply a fall from grace. But, before we accept that conclusion, we need to consider two important questions: (1) to what extent can perfect competition be accurately described as an ideal state? (2) what are the positive and negative features, from a welfare point of view, of the alternative forms of competition described above?

THE OPTIMALITY OF PERFECT COMPETITION

It is unnecessary to repeat here the standard arguments demonstrating that, even under the most perfect conditions of competition, there can be two serious deviations from optimality. The first is the existence of uncompensated externalities. The second is the impossibility of changing the distribution of income without imposing differential taxes on either income or expenditure, and thus inevitably undermining the marginal equalities established by perfect competition. (The alternative suggestion of income-redistributing lump sum taxes, assessed without regard either to income or expenditure, can hardly be taken seriously.)

But these two possible defects of perfect competition do not exhaust its weaknesses. In the first place, since perfect competition is inherently static, it is a system that provides no incentive for economic progress. When all technology is 'given', and therefore known by all, there can be no differences between firms in that respect. All firms automatically operate on the frontier of their production functions; and there can be no 'X-inefficiency'. Moreover, when technology it given from outside, there is no incentive, and indeed no sense, in a firm trying to improve its own technology. Since, in addition, there is no future (or no expectation of change in the future), there is no further role for the entrepreneur as a risk-taker. Apart from passive responses to exogenous changes in tastes, resources, or technology (which are strictly incompatible with the absence of uncertainty), perfect competition is essentially a condition of perfect stagnation.

These considerations suggest that it is necessary to reconsider the concept of 'optimality'. In its conventional usage the discussion of optimality is an attempt to answer the following question: Under what system of laws and government policies can we ensure that, with given resources and given technology, the economic system will produce the maximum alternative combinations of goods and services? In other words, how can we ensure that the economic system is 'allocatively efficient', that it stands on the frontier of its production possibilities? Although this is the basic question, a further stage in the inquiry may be to ascertain under what conditions these maximum production possibilities will be used to provide 'maximum' social satisfaction, defined as a Pareto-optimum in which it is impossible to make one person better off without making someone else worse off. The answer to both these questions is, of course, that, provided that there are no uncompensated externalities, the optimal system is perfect competition.

What is striking about this definition of optimality is that the definition itself presupposes static conditions, which has the effect of biasing the answer towards perfect competition and of excluding any system which incorporates endogenous technical progress, uncertainty, and a role for the entrepreneur. But there is no good reason why we should accept this definition of optimality. An alternative definition would be one which invites an answer to the following question: What system of laws and government policies is most likely to increase the productivity of labour over time, ensure that the average standard of living steadily rises, that wide opportunities are given to innovators and people of talent, and that sufficient resources can be raised by taxation to provide essential infrastructure, social services, and transfers to the poor? The answering of this question would direct attention not only to the means of achieving static allocative efficiency, but also to the means of achieving the highest possible level of 'X-efficiency', and the most rapid possible technical progress. The answer to this question, I maintain, would no longer be perfect competition.

We have so far left on one side another essential ingredient of a useful definition of optimality. That is that the question should be limited to economic systems that are 'feasible'. As we have shown in previous chapters, perfect competition is not a system which satisfies that criterion. There is no conceivable method of creating a real system in which technical knowledge is freely available to all, in which there is perfect knowledge of the qualities of borrowers, and perfect knowledge of the future. Yet all of these are assumed or implied in the model of perfect competition.

The nearest feasible alternative to perfect competition is the system which I have called 'semi-perfect competition'. In that system, there is still atomistic competition in product markets, but firms in a given industry vary in their technical knowledge, in their size, in their profitability, and in their rates of growth. Moreover, the entrepreneur, who generates internal technical progress and growth, is back in the picture. In this system, although in short-run equilibrium marginal cost for each firm is equal to the market price of its product, *long-run* marginal cost is not equal to that price (nor to the long-run equilibrium price). This means that, in comparison with a perfectly competitive world, the structure of industry is unsatisfactory, since most (or all) firms are of sub-optimal size, their costs are higher that they would be in such an ideal world, and the available resources are allocated in a sub-optimal manner. These defects carry over also to fixprice competition where, in addition, short-run marginal costs are usually less than prices, while differentiation encourages large expenditures on advertising and marketing.

In practice, we are left with two feasible system of competition: semi-perfect competition and fixprice competition. Let us proceed, therefore, to consider the social costs and benefits of each of these.

Despite the fact that perfect competition is not a feasible system, its domination of economic thought has been such that we shall include it also in the comparison.

A WELFARE COMPARISON OF SYSTEMS OF COMPETITION

It should now be obvious that economic systems cannot be judged by a single criterion. I would suggest that the criteria that should be included in an overall judgment should include: allocative efficiency; the rate of technical progress; the degree of stability of the system, since an unstable system increases uncertainty and leads to a waste of resources; the inflationary bias of the system; the degree of pretax income inequality generated by the system; and the extent to which income inequality can be altered through taxation without causing substantial adverse effects on efficiency and growth. For simplicity, we may call these six criteria: allocative efficiency; technical progress; stability; inflationary bias; pretax inequality; and taxability. We shall now attempt to rank the three systems of competition (perfect, semi-perfect, and fixprice) on these criteria.

On the criterion of allocative efficiency perfect competition (without major externalities) is the clear winner. Semi-perfect competition comes second, because in that system long-run marginal costs deviate from prices. And fixprice competition comes third, because in that system short-run marginal costs are also below price. On the criterion of technical progress, the ranking puts both semi-perfect and fixprice competition ahead of perfect competition, since in both semi-perfect and fixprice competition firms have an incentive to improve their private technology. This incentive is probably greater in the case of fixprice competition, where firms can expect to retain for at least some period a near-monopoly of their product designs and marketing techniques. On these grounds, fixprice competition seems to be the most technically progressive system; and experience supports this conclusion.

The criterion of stability has two dimensions: price stability and quantity stability. It can also be considered within two contexts:

microeconomic stability and macroeconomic stability. Microeconomic stability does not mean that there are no changes in relative prices or quantities, but rather that there is no tendency to 'overshoot' in such adjustments. All microeconomic adjustments are assumed to be relative to other firms or industries, and therefore real. Changes in the general levels of prices or quantities are regarded as macroeconomic. We may start by considering the microeconomic stability of each system, and then consider its macroeconomic stability.

When there is a change in relative demand or supply conditions, a perfectly competitive system will respond by immediate changes in relative prices, followed by changes in relative quantities. In principle, in long-run equilibrium there will be little change in relative prices and almost all the adjustment will made in quantities. But the initial changes in prices may (and indeed should) induce large inflows or outflows of competing firms seeking to maximize their profits (or minimize their losses); and these movements may produce an unstable 'cobweb' pattern of adjustment. Under semi-perfect competition, prices will be similarly unstable in the short run, but these fluctuations will not induce such large changes in supply conditions, since the new entrant or exit firms will be mainly small. Although firms already in each industry will tend to overshoot in their investment decisions, the absence of a perfect capital market will act as a restraining influence in comparison with the hypothetical perfect availability of capital under perfect competition. In general, therefore, while there will be some tendency to overshoot under conditions of semi-perfect competition, it may be expected to be less than under perfect competition. The most stable system, from a microeconomic point of view, is likely to be fix-price competition. In that system each firm has its own list of differentiated products and its own markets. Exogenous changes in supply conditions are not usually important, and changes in demand conditions will be met mainly or exclusively by changes in quantities produced by existing firms. Since each firm has its own market (or markets) it will expand or contract its capacity only to the degree necessary to satisfy its expected demand. There will be a much smaller tendency to overshoot that under either perfect of semi-perfect competition.

Changes in macroeconomic conditions may be defined as changes in nominal expenditures at a rate different from changes in aggregate real output. For simplicity, we may concentrate on the case of excessive increases in nominal expenditures, which is the most common under modern conditions. Under perfect competition such excess expenditures will affect all markets equally, and at the same speed (instantaneously). Prices of both final products and factors of production will increase in the same proportion, but quantities will be unchanged. Under conditions of semi-perfect competition, however, while markets for products will still respond immediately to excess nominal demand, imperfect markets for the factors – especially labour – will tend to create a time lag in the adjustment of wages. So long as that time lag lasts, there will be an artificial stimulus to aggregate output. But this will cease when (and if) wage increases catch up with the initial price increases.

By contrast, the initial reaction of firms in fixprice competition to excess nominal demand will be no change in prices but an increase in output. However, this will soon feed through into prices, since fixprice firms buy materials, directly or indirectly, from firms operating under conditions of semi-perfect competition. There may also be some upward pressure on prices as fixprice firms approach their capacity limits. (In an open economy, also, excess nominal demand will tend to reduce the value of the domestic currency, leading to a rise in the nominal prices of imported materials and final products.) As prices rise, there will be successful pressure for increases in nominal wages, which will be passed on in further increases in prices. Thus, unlike in the other two systems, fixprice competition responds to an initial excess nominal demand by starting a self-perpetuating inflationary spiral, which can be halted only by firm action to reduce nominal demand.

In the light of the above discussion it is difficult to make a firm ranking of the three systems on the criterion of stability. Prices, of both products and factors, respond most rapidly to changes in market conditions under perfect competition, while factor prices respond with a time lag under semi-perfect competition. And both systems have a tendency to overshoot. Fixprice competition, on the other hand, is slower to adjust prices, but faster in its adjustment of outputs. In addition, fixprice competition has an unpleasant tendency to convert an initial excess nominal demand into a self-perpetuating inflationary spiral. But this last characteristic may be classified under the next criterion: inflationary bias. If that is done, the stability ranking seems to give the first place to fixprice competition, followed by semi-perfect competition, with perfect competition last.

On the criterion of inflationary bias, for the reasons already given, fixprice competition comes last. There is not much to choose between the other two systems; but the existence of an imperfect labour market in semi-perfect competition creates a possibility of an inflationary bias, which would be absent in the perfect world of perfect competition.

The rankings of the last two criteria seem to be in opposite directions. The degree of pretax inequality is likely to be greatest in fixprice competition, in which firms (and their employees) enjoy the rents of their private technology and marketing expertise. Some technological rents, but on a smaller scale, also arise in semi-perfect competition; while in perfect competition, by assumption, such rents are excluded. On the other hand, the very fact that much of the profits and higher personal incomes generated under semi-perfect and fixprice competition is the result of a temporary technological or marketing monopoly makes it possible to impose fairly considerable company profits taxes and progressive income taxes without too seriously weakening the incentive to improve technology and to invest. The extent to which these taxes can be pushed without major adverse consequences on the rate of economic growth seems to vary from one country to another, depending on the strength of the entrepreneurial spirit in each country. For a long time Sweden has grown rapidly in spite of very high taxes, although this period now seems to be drawing to a close. Countries which are in the early stages of economic growth, when the encouragement of entrepreneurship is vital to success, cannot afford to tax away company profits to the same extent as countries which have a well-established entrepreneurial class. And 'old' countries, in which the entrepreneurial spirit has lost some of its early vigour, should also be careful not to use their more advanced administrative techniques to impose rates of profits taxes that further weaken the incentive (and the ability) to take risks.

CONCLUSIONS

The conclusions from the above comparisons are summarized in Table 5.1, in which each of the three systems is given a rank number in respect of each of the six criteria.

TABLE 5.1 *Ranking of alternative systems of competition*

	Perfect competition	Semi-perfect competition	Fixprice competition
Allocative efficiency	1	2	3
Technical progress	3	2	1
Stability	3	2	1
Inflationary bias	1	2	3
Pretax inequality	1	2	3
Taxability	3	2	1

Although the ranking of the three systems of competition gives different results for the different criteria, they suggest some useful conclusions. First, we find that, perhaps not surprisingly, semi-perfect competition is in the middle on all six rankings. Secondly, if we compare perfect competition with fixprice competition, the former wins on three criteria – allocative efficiency, inflationary bias, and pretax inequality – while the latter wins on the other three – technical progress, stability, and taxability. This comparison, of course, has no operational significance, since perfect competition is not an available choice. But it give some indication of the gains and losses of moving from a hypothetical economic paradise into the real modern world of predominantly fixprice competition. We may move on, thirdly, to make a comparison between semi-perfect competition and fixprice competition. While semi-perfect competition is ranked higher on three criteria – allocative efficiency, inflationary bias, and pretax inequality; fixprice competition is ranked higher on the other three criteria – technical progress, stability, and taxability.

We are not, of course, offered a free choice between these two systems. Free competitive development of a market economy has led to the evolution of fixprice competition out of semi-perfect competition, and there is no practicable way back. But, as in the comparison with perfect competition, it is interesting to know what we have gained and what we have lost. While it would be foolish to claim that we live in the best possible of worlds, humanity has surely benefitted enormously from the technical progress of the past two hundred years. And much of this progress has been associated with, and conditional upon, the shift from semi-perfect competition to fixprice competition.

The central argument of this book is that this extraordinary rate of economic development would never have occurred in the absence of the private technology created by competing private enterprises. Scientific discoveries are essential to economic development, but they are necessary, not sufficient, conditions. Recent experience has shown conclusively that countries which excel at science but neglect or disparage enterprise lag behind, while countries which have a multitude of dynamic entrepreneurs forge ahead, making use of the scientific discoveries and public technology of others. In Chapter 6, therefore, we shall turn to a closer examination of the role of the entrepreneur; and in Chapter 7 we shall consider the factors that influence the supply of entrepreneurs.

6 The Role of the Entrepreneur

Given their reliance on the model of perfect competition, it is not surprising that few economists have devoted much attention to the role of the entrepreneur. Many textbooks of microeconomics, or price theory, do not even mention entrepreneurship. General textbooks of economics, which are more eclectic, usually say something about the entrepreneur; but only to provide summaries of alternative views about his role. Entrepreneurship is a subject that is never integrated into the body of neoclassical theory, since it is, of course, logically impossible to do so. But a few well-known economists have addressed themselves to the subject; and we shall consider their views below. First, however, it is necessary to focus on the nature of the problem that needs to be explained.

THE SOURCES OF ECONOMIC GROWTH

During the past 120 years the productivity of labour in the countries that are now most industrially developed has risen at an unprecedented rate. According to estimates compiled by Angus Maddison, real gross domestic product per manhour increased between 1870 and 1977 in major countries of Western Europe by factors ranging from 5.7 for the United Kingdom to 20.4 for Sweden. The corresponding factors for France, Germany, and Italy were in the range of 13 to 15. The figure for Japan is an astonishing 24.6, and for the United States 11.4. If these estimates are approximately updated to 1990, the estimated United Kingdom increase in 120 years is over sevenfold, the factors for France, Germany, and Italy are in the range of 18 to 19, the Japanese figure rises to nearly 40, and the United States factor is about 14.[1] The astonishing rate of increase of labour productivity in Japan is clearly in part the result of a 'catch up' in technology and amount of capital per worker, as also in Sweden. In 1970 both these countries were relatively less developed. The low rate of growth of the United Kingdom can also be partly explained on the grounds that it started from a leading position in 1870. Perhaps the best estimate of potential growth in productivity in these 120 years, regardless of a country's initial position, would be the figure for the United States, which was at the frontier of technology for most of the period.

Much of these increases in productivity must, of course, be attributed to the great increases in this period in stocks of capital equipment per worker, and to improvements in the education and training of workers. It would be useful to know what proportion of the increases in productivity was due to these increases in nonhuman and human capital per worker, and what proportion to improvements in technology. But this is a difficult question to answer precisely, partly because there is no unique measure of a stock of capital, and partly because there is no certain method of estimating the effects of an increase in the stock of capital per worker on output per worker *in the absence of any change in technology*.

The best known, and to my mind the most impressive, attempts to answer this question have been made by Edward Denison.[2] In the second of the two studies referred to above, Denison estimated the average annual rate of growth of United States nonresidential business income per worker in the period 1929–1969 at 2.14 per cent, of which only 0.33 per cent was attributable to increases in the quantity and quality of labour (adjusted for hours of work) and in the stock of physical capital per worker (Table 8.4 in Denison). These estimates imply, therefore, that more than four-fifths of the growth in nonresidential business income per worker in this period was due to causes other than the increase in human and nonhuman capital per worker. Denison attempted to distribute this 'residual' over several identifiable causes, in particular, improved resource allocation (transfer of labour from less productive occupations to more productive) and economies of scale. His ultimate residual, which he described as 'advances in knowledge and not elsewhere classified', amounted to 1.10 per cent per annum, or about half of the total rate of increase in output per worker.

Similar estimates by Denison and Poullier for the United States and eight western European countries for the period 1950–62 suggest that in that period inputs of labour, capital and land per employed worker accounted for about one-third of the growth of national income per worker in the United States, and for about one-fifth of the growth of national income per worker in western Europe.[3] All these estimates tend, therefore, to confirm that only a minor part of the increases in total output per worker in industrialized countries in recent decades can be attributed to increases in human and nonhuman capital per worker.

This conclusion has been challenged by some other economists, who have concentrated their criticisms mainly on the method of estimating the stock of capital. They point out that Denison's estimates of the capital stock are based on cost of production, whereas the value of the services of capital depends on its quality. If the capital stock estimates could be adjusted by some satisfactory method to allow for improvements in quality, they would undoubtedly show a much greater increase in capital per worker than in Denison's estimates. And this would imply a much lower estimate of the importance of technical progress. In effect, such quality-adjusted estimates would include 'embodied' technical progress in the capital stock, leaving only 'disembodied' technical progress in the residual. If such an exercise could be carried out with any degree of reliability, its results would undoubtedly be interesting. But the fundamental difficulty is that adjustments of the capital stock for its quality are either arbitrary or circular, incorporating in the quality of capital most or all of the results of technical progress. There is no conceivable objective method, for example, by which we can compare the quality of the capital embodied in a modern aeroplane with the quality of the capital embodied in a horse and cart.

In any case, the separation of embodied from disembodied technical progress is not important for the present discussion. Both kinds of technical progress are the consequence of some activity of human agents other than increasing the 'physical' stocks of labour and capital. If the total effect of both these kinds of technical progress on output per worker have been of the orders of magnitude estimated by Denison, economic theory is confronted by a major problem of accounting for the importance of this crucial factor in economic growth.

The character and magnitude of the problem may be illustrated in two other ways. First, as a mental experiment, let us ask ourselves how much economic growth would have occurred in the past 250 years if all the extra investment in capital had consisted of additions to the stocks of structures and machines of exactly the same types as those that existed at the start of the period. By now we should have more canals, more unpaved roads, more horses and horse-drawn vehicles, more spinning wheels and handlooms, more scythes and horse-drawn ploughs, more sailing ships, and so forth. If the total stock of these forms of capital had increased faster than the labour force, its marginal productivity would have fallen, and its contribution to growth would have been that much reduced. A rough measure of the importance of technical progress over this period would be to compare output per worker as it actually is with what it would have been in the conditions of our mental experiment. Clearly, the difference would be enormous.

Secondly, we may compare the rates of growth of different countries during the past 40 years. Every one now knows that the continental members of the European Community and certain countries of east Asia (Japan, South Korea, Taiwan, Hong Kong, and Singapore) have grown much faster than most other countries. The fast growers have had high investment ratios but, even when this is taken into account, there is a large residual attributable to technical progress. By way of comparison, the socialist countries have also had very high investment ratios (in both human and nonhuman capital), and have ended in a state of economic crisis, in some cases not even being able to feed their people adequately. There must be some unmeasured factor that has helped the fast growers, and whose absence has hindered the slow growers (and in the case of the socialist countries has led to a vast waste of scarce resources). That unmeasured factor is, quite clearly, technology. For the reasons given earlier, I maintain that most of these advances in applied technology are the results of the activity of entrepreneurs.

With this background in mind, we may now attempt to identify more precisely what role is played by the entrepreneur. We shall start by examining the views of four well-known economists who have worked on this problem. After that, we shall be able to draw some conclusions, relating them to the ideas advanced in earlier chapters.

THE VIEWS OF FOUR ECONOMISTS

Alfred Marshall[4]

Marshall does not use the term 'entrepreneur', but usually 'business man', sometimes also 'employer', 'undertaker', or – in appropriate cases – 'manufacturer'. His main emphasis is on the role of the business man as an *organizer of production* (*Principles of Economics*, p. 293). While recognizing that some business men are mainly engaged in speculation, e.g. as dealers on the stock exchange, he does not consider them to be as socially useful as those who organize production. Marshall lists a number of the qualities required of a manufacturer who produces goods for general sale. First, he must have 'a thorough knowledge of *things* in his own trade. He must have the power of forecasting the broad movements of production and consumption, of seeing where there is an opportunity for supplying a new commodity that will meet a real want or improving the plan of producing an old commodity. He must be able to judge cautiously and undertake risks boldly; and he must of course understand the materials and machinery used in his trade' (ibid., p. 297). Secondly, in his role of employer the business man 'must be a natural leader of men. He must have the power of first choosing his assistants rightly and then trusting them fully; of interesting them in the business and of getting them to trust him, so as to bring out whatever enterprise and power of origination there is in them' (ibid., pp. 297–8). Thirdly, the business man must exercise 'a general control over everything', and preserve 'order and unity in the main plan of the business' (ibid., p. 298).

Turning to more analytical aspects of the business man's role, Marshall suggests that he has three functions: (1) to supply part or all of the capital of the business; (2) to use his 'business ability', or 'business power', in managing the business; and (3) to 'bring together' these two contributions, thus creating 'business ability in command of capital'. Each of these functions is assumed to have a supply price, called respectively 'interest', 'net earnings of management', and 'gross earnings of management' (ibid., p. 313). While Marshall mentions in passing at various points in his extensive discussion of business management that business men take risks, this aspect of their role is not given much prominence. The first edition of his book was published in 1890, and his description of the role of the business man has a late-Victorian English flavour. Business men are depicted preeminently as serious, hard-working, conscientious men, whose main task is to ensure that their businesses are kept up to a high level of efficiency (what would now be called a high level of 'X-efficiency'). Although a business man may know a good deal about the standard technology of his business, Marshall does not give him a special role as a pioneer of new technology (either physical or organizational). He may become a 'leader of men', but hardly a 'captain of industry'.

There is much sound sense in Marshall's description of the development of business organization; but he does not address explicitly the crucial question of the importance of the business man's third function – the joint supply of business ability and capital. Marshall points out that 'experience shows operative ideas and experiments in business technique, and in business organization, to be rare in Government undertakings, and not very common in private enterprises which have drifted towards bureaucratic methods as a result of their great age and size' (ibid., p. 304); and this gives a hint of the special role of the dynamic private business man. But Marshall does not pursue this point. In commenting on the 'one great source of weakness' of joint stock companies he concentrates on the inability of shareholders to ensure strict labour discipline and the prevention of fraud (ibid., p. 303). Marshall does not develop a theory to account for the fact that a combination of business ability and capital yields, at least in some cases, much higher returns than could be imputed from adding together interest on loan capital and the earnings of management. For this purpose, he would have needed to have given more attention to the role of risk and uncertainty, as well as to the special incentives and opportunities that are created when a man of business ability finds himself in command of a significant sum of capital.

Frank Knight[5]

Knight's principal concern was to account for the existence of profit, and this led him to consider the role of entrepreneurship. He started by pointing out that under perfect competition, with perfect knowledge and hence a static (or stationary) state, all prices would be equal to costs, and there would be no profits or losses. Since there would be no new decisions to be made, there would be no role for the entrepreneur (*Risk, Uncertainty and Profit*, p. 18). Knight also suggested that steady growth, in which the future can be foreseen, would be compatible with an equilibrium of perfect competition. The only changes, therefore, which give rise to profits or losses are those which are irregular, unforeseen, and hence uncertain (ibid., pp. 37–8).

Knight devotes considerable attention to the analysis of uncertainty. He makes a distinction between risk, which arises when there is a known probability distribution of outcomes; and uncertainty, which exists when the parameters of that probability distribution are unknown, and consequently have to be estimated by the decision-maker on the basis of fragmentary information. A typical example of risk is life insurance since, for specified classes of persons, the empirically recorded probability of death at various ages appears to be stable. At the other pole is a business decision made in an apparently unique set of circumstances (ibid., Chap VII). The true basis of Knight's distinction between risk and uncertainty is the size and variation of the sample of observations on the basis of which the parameters of the probability distribution have been estimated. All empirically-based estimates of such parameters have a standard error of estimate, the size of which depends on the size of the sample and its internal variance. Even in the case of life insurance the estimates of these parameters are subject to some uncertainty. Nevertheless, it is true that the estimates made in business (and most other) decision-making are usually based on very small samples of relevant experience, with much internal variance, and are therefore subject to a high degree of uncertainty.

According to Knight, in cases where there is abundant previous experience, the decision-maker is faced only with risk, or 'measurable uncertainty' (ibid., p. 233), and this can be included in the cost of production by various methods, such as insurance or diversification. If this is done, there will be no residue of profit or loss. Profit or loss arise only where there is 'unmeasurable uncertainty', which compels the decision-maker to rely on his own judgement. The exercise of such judgement is, in Knight's opinion, the primary task of the entrepreneur. People differ widely in their capacity to form correct judgements about the future course of events, about human nature, and about methods of achieving their objectives. They also differ in their degree of confidence in their own judgements, and in their general attitude to taking risks (their degree of risk-aversion) (ibid., pp. 241–2). As a consequence, there is a growth of specialization, with entrepreneurs accepting the responsibility for 'uncertainty-bearing' and employees preferring to work under the direction of entrepreneurs for fixed wages (ibid., pp. 244–5).

Uncertainty-bearing means making decisions under conditions of uncertainty about their outcome. In the absence of uncertainty there would be no decisions to be made, and hence no function for the decision-makers (ibid., p. 268). But there is ultimately an inseparable connection between making industrial decisions and taking the consequences of those decisions (ibid., p. 260). So it becomes the responsibility of the entrepreneur to exercise control over the implementation of decisions. 'The essence of enterprise is the specialization of the function of *responsible direction* of economic life, the neglected feature of which is the inseparability of these *two* elements, *responsibility* and *control*.' This function is carried out by entrepreneurs, 'a special social class', who 'direct economic activity' (ibid., p. 271).

The entrepreneur's income, profit or loss, is a residual. It is what remains after the incomes of the other factors, with fixed incomes, have been paid (ibid., p. 280). The level of profit depends on the entrepreneur's capacity; on his judgment of his own capacity; and on his luck (ibid., p. 281). In order to succeed, an entrepreneur needs also the 'power to give satisfactory guarantees', which means access to sufficient capital (ibid., p. 283). Normally, this means that the entrepreneur must himself supply a minimum part of this capital, although 'demonstrated ability can always get funds for business operations' (ibid., p. 274n). Knight is never quite sure whether entrepreneurs need to have a minimum amount of their own capital to start with. 'Demonstrated ability' clearly does not solve the problem, since a potential entrepreneur has, by definition, not yet had an opportunity to demonstrate his business ability.

'To find men capable of managing business efficiently and secure to them the positions of responsible control is perhaps the most important single problem of economic organization on the efficiency side' (ibid., p. 283). In the larger enterprise '"control" consists mainly of selecting someone else to do the "controlling". Business judgment is chiefly judgment of men' (ibid., p. 291). Similarly, 'The *crucial* decision . . . is the selection of men to make decisions'. Other sorts of decision-making or exercise of judgement are 'automatically reduced to a routine function' (ibid., p. 297). This function of personnel selection goes down through each layer of the organization, and constitutes the principal form of decision-making by managers at each level. Hence, 'The ability to judge men in relation to the problems they are to deal with, and the power to "inspire" them to efficiency in judging other men and things, are the essential characteristic of the executive' (ibid., p. 311).

Knight maintains that 'The responsible decisions in organized economic life are price decisions; others can be reduced to routine and men can be hired to make them'. Moreover, 'the main uncertainty which affects the entrepreneur is that connected with the sale price of his product' (ibid., p. 317). Although Knight sometimes makes a passing reference to the importance of technology and organizational efficiency, he does not allot to the entrepreneur any special role in improving these. He seems to have carried over from the model of perfect competition the idea that technology is 'given'. His criticism of that model is essentially confined to its neglect of the uncertainty arising from changes in circumstances, i.e. its failure to recognize the absence of perfect knowledge of the future. He does not notice the equally important absence of perfect knowledge of technology.

Two of Knight's other conclusions are of particular interest. First, he points out that special abilities are needed in order to manage large enterprises successfully, and that the rewards for this activity are correspondingly large (ibid., p. 283). Secondly, his theory about the distribution of aggregate income between profits and other incomes is that the share of profit depends on two factors: the supply of 'entrepreneur ability', and the rapidity of diminishing returns to the other factors of production (ibid., pp. 284–5). This conclusion, it should be noted, is essentially neoclassical, and depends on the operation of a system of perfect competition, which he had previously criticized and rejected.

Joseph Schumpeter

Schumpeter discussed the role of the entrepreneur in two of his books – *The Theory of Economic Development* and *Capitalism, Socialism, and Democracy* – published with an interval of thirty years. While the views expressed in both books are essentially the same, the second contains some small amendments, as well as additional comments on related matters. References will, therefore, be made to both books, starting with the first.[6] In the references below the first book will be called *Theory* and the second *Capitalism*.

Schumpeter started from the same position as Knight, namely that the model of perfect competition works only in a changeless static, or stationary, state. In such conditions, as Walras had noted long before, there would be no role for entrepreneurs, and there would be no profits or losses. This implies that entrepreneurship comes into existence only when the economic system is subject to change (*Theory*, pp. 21–2 and 31). But whereas Knight emphasized the effect of change on the creation of uncertainty, Schumpeter concentrated his attention on bringing out the causes of economic change. According to the 'traditional view', he remarked, improvement is 'something which just happens'. But changes in technique and in productive organization 'require special analysis'. 'The non-recognition of this is the most important single reason for what appears unsatisfactory to us in economic theory' (*Theory*, p. 60n).

Schumpeter makes a distinction between 'continuous' changes, such as the gradual emergence of a 'great department store out of a small retail business', which, he maintains, can be analysed by static methods, and 'revolutionary' changes. By 'development' he proposes to mean only the latter type of changes or, more specifically, 'only such changes in economic life as are not forced upon it from without but arise by its own initiative, from within' (*Theory*, pp. 62–3). He further defines development as 'carrying out new combinations', of which there are five cases: introducing a new good, introducing a new method of production, opening a new market, finding a new source of supply of materials or goods, and establishing a new method or organization, such as either creating or breaking up a monopoly (*Theory*, p. 66). When a firm makes one of these changes successfully, it is able to raise its prices or reduce its costs, and thus make profits. But this advantage is only temporary (except presumably in his fifth case), since other firms sooner or later make similar changes, and the profits are competed away. In this way society ultimately benefits from profit-maximizing changes initiated by individuals (*Theory*, p. 133).

New combinations are made by entrepreneurs. They may also be the owners or managers, but they are not identical with either category (*Theory*, p. 75). 'The entrepreneur's essential function must always appear mixed up with other kinds of activity, which as a rule must be much more conspicuous than the essential one' (*Theory*, p. 77). When an entrepreneur is not 'making new combinations' but, after building up his business, 'settles down to running it as other people run their businesses', he ceases to be an entrepreneur (*Theory*, p. 78). With such a 'dynamic' view of their function, Schumpeter regards entrepreneurs as people of exceptional intellect and will (*Theory*, p. 82n). But once they have established a routine, there is no further need to exercise their powers of leadership. 'Of course, it is still necessary to set people their tasks, to keep up discipline, and so forth; this is easy and a function any normal person can learn to fulfil' (*Theory*, p. 84). It is clear that, at least at the time when he wrote that last statement, Schumpeter could not have had the experience of holding a responsible administrative position.

Schumpeter argues that entrepreneurial innovation can be financed only by the expansion of credit (*Theory*, p. 70). He also maintains that 'The entrepreneur is never the risk bearer'. 'Even though he may risk his reputation, the direct responsibility of failure never falls on him.' Risk is borne by those who supply the capital, principally the creditors. Even if the entrepreneur supplies part of the capital, he does so in his capacity of capitalist, not as entrepreneur (*Theory*, p. 137).

In his later book, which is more of a political tract than a work of economic theory, Schumpeter made use of his earlier ideas about the role of the entrepreneur, but to some extent sharpened them by the employment of more colourful language. The 'essential fact about capitalism', he now suggested, is that it is 'a process of Creative

Destruction' (*Capitalism*, p. 83). The function of the entrepreneur 'is to reform or revolutionize the pattern of production by exploiting an invention or, more generally, an untried technological possibility for producing a new commodity or producing an old one in a new way, by opening up a new source of supply of materials or a new outlet for products, by reorganizing an industry and so on ... This function does not essentially consist in either inventing anything or otherwise creating the conditions which the enterprise exploits. It consists in getting things done' (*Capitalism*, p. 132).

But this social function 'is already losing importance and is bound to lose it at an accelerating rate in the future', because 'innovation is being reduced to routine', and 'technological progress is increasingly becoming the business of teams of trained specialists'. 'Thus, economic progress tends to become depersonalized and automatized. Bureau and committee work tends to replace individual action' (*Capitalism*, pp. 132–3). As a result, the entrepreneur becomes redundant, and capitalism itself goes the same way. 'Since capitalist enterprise, by its very achievements, tends to automatize progress, we conclude that it tends to make itself superfluous.' The bourgeoisie is 'expropriated' by the 'perfectly bureaucratized giant industrial unit', which also eliminates all small and medium-sized firms (*Capitalism*, p. 134). Schumpeter concluded that socialism is inevitable and that, in particular, its acceptance was rapidly approaching in 'England', where the people 'on the whole have become state-broken' (*Capitalism*, p. 229).

We shall reserve our comments on this later development of Schumpeter's thought until the final section of this chapter. But it will already be obvious to the reader that Schumpeter's fifty-year-old prognosis was faulty. In this respect, of course, he was in good company with most eminent economists who have ventured to forecast the distant future.

Israel Kirzner

In recent years Kirzner has been a leading contributor to the debate on the role of the entrepreneur.[7] Working in the 'Austrian' tradition of Mises and Hayek, Kirzner emphasizes the absence of perfect knowledge, without which there is no necessary equilibrium of perfect competition. If such an equilibrium in fact existed, there would be no role in it for the entrepreneur (*Competition and Entrepreneurship*, p. 26). But normally, indeed – as will be seen below – at all times, there is a state of disequilibrium, in which there are unexploited opportunities for making profits. It is the entrepreneur who, by his 'alertness', discovers these profitable opportunities and, by following them up, brings the economy closer to a state of competitive equilibrium (ibid., pp. 13–14).

The entrepreneur is not a simple 'maximizer', facing 'given' ends and means, but a '*homo agens*', as postulated by Mises. He discovers new ends and new means. He has 'drive' and 'alertness' (ibid., pp. 33–4). Kirzner defines 'the entrepreneurial element' as 'alertness to possibly new worthwhile goals and to possibly newly available resources'. This element makes human action 'active, creative, and human rather than passive, automatic, and mechanical' (ibid., p. 35).

Kirzner maintains that a pure entrepreneur has no need to possess any other resources, because he can hire 'all the talent needed to organize factors of production into a smoothly working team'. He is not, therefore, a 'producer' in the normal sense (ibid., p. 45). Because of the absence of need for additional resources, *everyone* is a potential entrepreneur, provided that he has the necessary quality of alertness to profitable opportunities (ibid., p. 17). This alertness is apparently not directed towards possible technical or organizational improvements but exclusively towards price discrepancies. 'Pure entrepreneurial profit is the difference between two sets of prices' (ibid., p. 48). Moreover, entrepreneurship does not consist in having superior knowledge, but in 'knowing where to look for knowledge' (ibid., p. 68).

Kirzner distinguishes his views from those of Schumpeter by saying that, while Schumpeter's entrepreneur breaks into a state of equilibrium, creating a temporary disequilibrium, his entrepreneur is constantly moving the economy *towards* equilibrium (ibid., pp. 72–3). His entrepreneur creates nothing '*ex nihilo*', but merely responds to existing opportunities (ibid., p. 74). 'For me the function of the entrepreneur consists not of *shifting* the curves of cost or of revenues which face him, *but of noticing that they have in fact shifted*' (ibid., p. 81). The implication is that all possible knowledge, including knowledge of technology, already exists, although much of it has not yet been brought to light. When someone discovers a new opportunity for profitable business activity, he is not 'creating' new knowledge, but only revealing what is already 'there'. Since, for all we know, the amount of possible knowledge is infinite, this means that we are always in a state of disequilibrium, and always will be. History, on this interpretation, is a gradual movement towards equilibrium.

It seems to me that the difference between Kirzner's view of development and the views of others, including Schumpeter, depends in part on the definition of the term 'equilibrium'. To my mind, Kirzner's definition is not helpful, because it obscures the very ideas that he himself wishes to promote, of the entrepreneur as an 'active, creative' human being. I consider, also, that the scope for entrepreneurial creativity goes beyond simply noticing price discrepancies and opportunities for arbitrage. It includes, for example, the creation of new technical, organizational, and marketing systems, and the building up of a team of responsive, efficient, and innovatory workers. These activities cannot be resolved into noticing price discrepancies, unless one were to assume that, with sufficient funds, one can always hire people and machines to do what is needed. But it is a fallacy to believe that the services of hired employees, and even of machines, will always come up to expectations without the constant supervision, leadership, and decision-making of the entrepreneur.

CONCLUSIONS

While, as is natural, there is a good deal of common ground in the views of the four economists summarized above, there are important differences of emphasis. The sharpest line of division is between Marshall and the other three on the question whether perfect competition is compatible with change. Marshall never accepted the Walrasian concept of general equilibrium, and consequently saw no incompatibility between competition and change. In any case, Marshall's business men were not of the dynamic type, making radical changes in products or processes, but solid, serious, honest, and respectable organizers of production. He seems to have thought of them, not as the instituters of 'revolutionary' changes, but rather as striving to achieve the maximum of 'X-efficiency' within a given technology. Marshall's business men supply both capital and management, and the secret of profit is somehow connected with this joint supply. But Marshall was not able to explain the matter any further. He did not ask why business men are obliged to supply part of the capital of their businesses, nor what he really meant by the phrase 'business ability'. Nevertheless, Marshall recognized that organizations like cooperatives which attempt to operate by hiring both capital and management, thus dispensing with the element of 'business ability', are generally not very efficient. One wonders why he did not ask himself precisely why this was so.

Each of the other three economists started from the recognition that perfect competition is incompatible with change (although Knight maintained that it is compatible with steady change). And each of them pointed to the principal difficulty in the model of perfect competition, namely, the assumption of perfect knowledge. But they differ in the types of knowledge whose imperfection they regard as crucial. Whereas Knight concentrated on imperfect knowledge of the future, Schumpeter focused on imperfect knowledge of technology, and Kirzner is mainly concerned with imperfect knowledge of market opportunities. But these three kinds of imperfect knowledge all stem from the same root, namely, imperfect knowledge of the effects of current decisions on future outcomes. Every change in technology, even the most elementary, including a 'short-run' decision to hire more labour or to use more materials, is a step into the unknown. Every discovery of what is believed to be a price discrepancy is a judgement about the future effects of decisions taken on the basis of that alleged discovery. And every decision to act on such a discovery, except in the case of a purely speculative transaction, involves the making of technical decisions, the effects of which are inevitably uncertain.

Both Schumpeter and Marshall considered that speculation is not part of strict entrepreneurship, while Knight and Kirzner make no such distinction. Indeed, Kirzner denies that the pure entrepreneur is involved in production. His only function is to discover (apparently) profitable market opportunities, after which he can, if he wishes, hire all the factors of production to carry out any production activities that are needed. This latter view was also held by Knight. But I have already pointed out the lack of realism of this assumption.

Schumpeter takes some rather extreme positions. He maintains, for example, that only 'revolutionary' changes in technology require the services of an entrepreneur. In most businesses, he believes, operations can be reduced to 'routine', and left in the charge of hired managers. (Kirzner agrees with this conclusion, although not with the premise on which it is based.) It was this view that led Schumpeter to accept the inevitability of socialism. What he overlooked, as the history of socialism (including partial socialization through nationalization) has shown, was that the potential supply of 'revolutionary' changes in technology has not dried up in the past fifty years but has rapidly increased; and that, even when there are no 'revolutionary' changes in technology, every business is constantly faced with changes in its environment and in its own composition (including the attitudes of its personnel), and that these changes require new entrepreneurial decisions if the business is to prosper, or even to survive. Any business that assumes that it can be run indefinitely by routine methods will stagnate, and eventually die. This is an application of the law of 'natural selection' in the business world.

Kirzner also takes the extreme position (partially accepted by Knight) that there is no reason in principle why the entrepreneur should supply any of the other factors of production, including capital. Here, it seems to me, he fails to recognize that all entrepreneurial decisions necessarily involve the *investment* of capital, i.e. the conversion of liquid capital into another asset or group of assets, whether financial or physical. It is this conversion of capital from one form to another that creates risk. (If all capital, like land, were lent *in specie*, this risk factor would be largely, although not entirely, eliminated. Even landowners need to monitor the uses that their tenants make of their property.) The lender of capital runs the risk that, if the borrower is dishonest or unsuccessful, part or all of his capital will be irrecoverable. That is why the wise lender insists that the borrower should both be of good reputation and invest part of the equity of the business from his own resources. Consequently, the need for the borrower to supply part of the equity is inescapable in the case of new entrants (who, by definition, have no established reputation), and even for medium-sized firms. Only in the case of the very large, well-established, firm, which has become a public company, do we find a tendency for the entrepreneurial function to be taken over to a large extent by appointed directors, who may even have no direct investment in the firm's equity, although their career prospects continue to be closely tied to the firm's success.[8]

While Knight also tends to take an extreme position, by concentrating almost all his attention on 'uncertainty-bearing' at the expense of the role of the entrepreneur as an innovator and organizer of production, he has many wise insights, the most important of which, in my opinion, is his recognition of the inevitable link between responsibility (arising from the right to make decisions) and control. This relation can work in both directions. The person (or group) who makes the ultimate decisions, which inevitably include putting capital at risk, carries the responsibility for the outcome of those decisions; and, for that reason, he (or they) can logically insist on the right of control. But, in the other direction, those who are given management control over resources can rightly be held responsible for the results of their decisions. If the system is such as to obstruct this connection, the inevitable result will be slackness, inefficiency, and waste of resources. All of these phenomena can be seen vividly at work in the socialist countries, where overmanning is on a colossal scale, and both stocks of goods and capital equipment are allowed to decay.

What, then, is the role of the entrepreneur? My own views, which have largely been implicit in comments made in this and previous chapters, may be summarized as follows:

1. An economic system, especially a modern industrialized economy, is so complex, has so many millions of products, and is subject to so much change, both in the short term and in the long term, that the only way in which it can be operated efficiently is through decentralized decision-making by business organizations, which we call 'firms'. So far as possible, decision-makers need to be in direct contact with those who are carrying out their decisions, so that there is constant control over the fulfilment of decisions, and constant feedback from all levels of the

organization to those at higher levels. As Hayek has especially emphasized, it is the people who are near the points of business operation who have most of the knowledge needed for making wise decisions. This information is supplemented by information about prices established in a competitive market, which provides decision-makers with a mass of important data that they could not obtain in any other way.[9]

2. In a complex economy, decentralization of business decision-making to individual firms is possible only in a market system; and the system can operate efficiently only if the decision-maker is forced to carry responsibility for the results of his decisions, which is possible only under capitalism. The person who makes these decisions is the 'entrepreneur'. Because he is operating in a market environment, his aim is to maximize his firm's profits. If we are interested mainly in the effects of entrepreneurship on economic growth, we can exclude from consideration firms or individuals who are solely engaged in speculation. This is not to deny that some kinds of speculation have either good or bad effects on economic growth. But there remains an important distinction between the pure speculator and the entrepreneur engaged in production of goods or services.
3. New entrepreneurs are, by definition, untried and have had no opportunity to acquire a good business reputation. Consequently, except when they can obtain capital from friends or relations, they will be obliged to provide most of their initial capital out of their own resources, or by using such resources as collateral for loans. This has two important effects. It limits the size of the new entrant firm, and it puts the owner's capital (and reputation) at risk. For the latter reason, it is inevitable that the owner should insist that he must have the ultimate power of decision-making and control.
4. In a world of change, all entrepreneurs suffer from imperfect knowledge. This takes various forms: imperfect knowledge of technology, imperfect knowledge of the market, and imperfect knowledge of the future effects of current decisions about these and other matters. Entrepreneurs who have superior knowledge in any of these respects will do better than others. They can

sometimes obtain such knowledge if they are more 'alert' to the possibilities of obtaining it, and if they make determined efforts to do so. Clearly, some people are more alert to business opportunities than others.

5. But even the most alert entrepreneur does not have *certain* knowledge. All that he has is expectations, which may be either strong or weak. Some entrepreneurs are more confident about the correctness of their expectations than others, and will consequently act more boldly. Some of these will be outstandingly successful; but others not. Because of the uncertainty of entrepreneurial expectations, many people who already have, or can obtain, the necessary capital to set up in business on their own account are reluctant to do so. This is especially the case if they have a choice of an alternative occupation in which they can earn a good and steady income, or with good pension prospects. The willingness to take risks is a necessary quality of the entrepreneur; but this willingness is not independent of the environment, and in particular of the alternative occupations available to him.
6. The range and quality of an entrepreneur's knowledge normally increases with experience. This applies especially to knowledge of technology. Technology is of two kinds: public and private. The former is available to all at little cost; the latter is possessed exclusively (for a certain period) by individual firms. Most of public technology was originally private, but became available to the public at large over time. What is 'public' in one country is not necessarily 'public' in another, because of differences of language and sources of information and instruction. Technology covers not only physical but also organizational methods, and it is particularly the latter type of technology that is the private property of firms. Private organizational technology, like physical technology, grows with experience, and the knowledge of how to operate efficiently on a large scale can normally be obtained only by experience of operating on a somewhat smaller scale. This is a major reason, in addition to the problem of obtaining the necessary capital, why new firms cannot expect to operate efficiently *ab initio* on a large scale.

7. Up to a certain size, because of economies of scale, larger firms make, on the average, more profits per unit of labour or capital than smaller firms; and this provides most firms with an incentive to grow. The profit prospects from reinvesting in the same line of business are usually better than the rate of interest obtainable by external lending; but larger and more experienced firms can sometimes use their private organizational 'know-how' successfully to diversify into new lines. But all decisions to expand or diversify are risky. Only entrepreneurs who are still ambitious, energetic, and self-confident will continue to make such decisions. In any one period, there are wide variations between firms, both in their profitability and their rates of growth. These variations depend on the nature of the industry, the size of firm, the ability of the entrepreneur, and pure chance.
8. In order to be successful, an entrepreneur must have a strong sense of commitment, and be prepared to work extremely hard, especially in the early stages of the development of his firm. He has to supervise every aspect of the firm's operation: the design of the product, choice of market, technology of production, raising of finance, control of accounts, and selection, training, and supervision of staff. He must be alert to all changes in any of these matters, and be ready to make new decisions to correct weaknesses. He must constantly check up on the implementation of his decisions. As he gets older his strength and enthusiasm may slacken, and eventually the problem of the succession will need to be solved. His ideal successor is usually someone who combines the inheritance of a large part of his fortune with ability, commitment, and a considerable experience in the business (thus equipping him with the requisite knowledge of the firm's private technology). But it is not always easy to find such a candidate. The heir to the fortune may not have the right abilities, or the right attitudes. If he has been over-indulged, or encouraged to pursue a purely academic kind of education, he may have become unsuitable to occupy his father's role. At this point, it may be decided that the best solution is to transfer the entrepreneurial role to the top management team, led by a managing director of their choice. The danger of this solution

is that such a self-replacing group of top managers will gradually lose flexibility and dynamism, and settle for a 'quiet life'. This danger may be in part avoided by giving managers profit incentives. The ultimate remedy, however, may be the threat, or actuality, of a shareholders' revolt or an external takeover.

9. In the long run, the most successful firms seem to be those in which the entrepreneur pays special attention to the selection and training of his managerial staff, indeed of all his employees. Such an entrepreneur organizes people efficiently, inspires them with interest in and loyalty towards the enterprise, and provides them with incentives to work well, to maintain standards of quality, and to bring forward innovatory ideas. In this way the entrepreneur ensures a rapid growth of his firm's private technology. Although he retains the ultimate capital risk, the entrepreneurial function is to a considerable extent shared by the whole staff, working as a team. The best modern exemplars of these methods are, of course, the Japanese. But some Western firms have shown similar characteristics in the past, and many are beginning to recognize the need to change their methods for the future.
10. Profits are not simply a reward for uncertainty-bearing, although it is true that many people prefer to avoid making decisions that may seriously affect their future prospects, especially when less uncertain alternatives are available to them. As a result, the supply of people willing to make major business decisions is limited, and the profits made by those who are prepared to make such decisions, *and who make successful decisions*, can be regarded as in part a rent of a scarce ability. But willingness to bear uncertainty is not a sufficient condition for making profits (as many investors in the stock market soon discover). The outcome of entrepreneurial decisions depends on all the abilities mentioned above. Profits are, therefore, a reward for (1) willingness to bear uncertainty, (2) the possession of sufficient resources, (3) a knowledge of the relevant technology, (4) a combination of special abilities, such as alertness to business opportunities, good judgement, self-confidence, leadership, ambition, and drive, (5) a large current input of work and worry,

and (6) good luck. For greatest success in business, all these qualities must be available in joint supply.

11. Those countries that have legal restrictions on private entrepreneurship, or in which entrepreneurship is discouraged by other means, tend to stagnate, and eventually move into a state of economic crisis. Examples of this process can be found among all types of country, developed and less developed market economies as well as socialist countries. There are, therefore, two conditions for economic progress. First, there must be freedom of enterprise, supported by an appropriate legal framework and an appropriate combination of government policies. Secondly, there must be a plentiful supply of good entrepreneurs. The problem of ensuring that this second condition is met will be the subject of Chapter 7.

7 The Supply of Entrepreneurship

In standard economic theory there is no significant role for the entrepreneur. At most he has the task of calculating marginal cost (or hiring someone else to do that) and equating it with price or marginal revenue. When considering investment projects, he must make estimates of future yields (or hire someone else to do that), apply a suitable discount factor, and compare the present value of the project with its cost. There is no obvious reason why there should be a shortage of people capable, under suitable instruction, of making such calculations. Consequently, in standard economic theory there is no need to consider whether entrepreneurship, like other factors, has a supply side. The implied assumption is that, provided that there is a suitable legal framework, a free market, and freedom of enterprise, there will be an ample – and virtually infinitely elastic – supply of entrepreneurs. It is sometimes said that new entrants expect to receive 'normal profits'. But this concept is never clarified, nor made consistent with the basic assumptions of perfect competition.

Naturally, the four economists whose views on the role of the entrepreneur were summarized in Chapter 6, also had something to say about the supply of entrepreneurship. But not very much. Marshall, writing in 1890, expressed the opinion that 'in modern England the supply of business ability in command of capital accommodates itself, as a general rule, to the demand for it; and thus has a fairly defined supply price' (*Principles*, p. 313). In addition, 'The supply of business power is large and elastic, since the area from which it is drawn is wide. Everyone has the business of his own life to conduct; and in this he can gain some training for business management, if he has the natural aptitudes for it' (ibid., p. 606). In another passage, however, he wrote 'The abilities required to make an ideal employer are so great and so numerous that very few persons can exhibit them all in a high degree' (ibid., p. 298). Marshall was also aware that the required abilities vary with the size of firm (ibid., p. 298 and p. 606).

Knight listed the qualities required of a successful entrepreneur as ability, willingness, 'power to give satisfactory guarantees', and 'the coincidence of these factors'; and he added that the 'ability to handle large enterprises successfully' is rare and tends to earn large rewards (*Risk, Uncertainty and Profit*, pp. 282-3). He also expressed the view that 'all men are competing for positions as entrepreneurs' (ibid., p. 273). But he did not go any further into the problem of supply.

Schumpeter considered that the only truly entrepreneurial decisions are those that lead to 'revolutionary' changes in business organization or activity, and that normal business management is 'routine'. 'To act with confidence beyond the range of familiar beacons, and to overcome [the resistance of the environment] requires aptitudes that are present in only a small fraction of the population' (*Capitalism, Socialism, and Democracy*, p. 132). But, since 'This function is already losing importance and is bound to lose it at an accelerating rate in the future', because 'innovation itself is being reduced to routine' and 'technological progress is increasingly becoming the business of trained specialists', the supply of entrepreneurship was not a matter to which Schumpeter thought it necessary to devote any great attention (ibid., p. 132).

Kirzner, on the other hand, considers that anyone who has the quality of 'alertness' can be an entrepreneur. He does not need to supply any other factor. This suggests that the supply of entrepreneurs is large and elastic. But Kirzner does not explore in detail the conditions that determine the supply of 'alertness'.

From this brief review, it seems fair to conclude that none of these four economists considered that the supply of entrepreneurship is, or could be, a problem. This conclusion clearly applies *a fortiori* to the great majority of economists, who do not even regard entrepreneurship as a factor of production. Entrepreneurs are of many different kinds. There are farmers, shopkeepers, manufacturers, bankers, and so on. They also vary according to the size of the enterprise which they control. In the final analysis, the supply of each of these different kinds of entrepreneur might be considered separately. In this brief introduction to the subject, however, it will be sufficient to distinguish two main types of entrepreneur: new and experienced entrepreneurs.

THE SUPPLY OF NEW ENTREPRENEURS

Since new entrepreneurs are derived from other sections of the population, one possible influence on their supply may be the magnitude of the groups from which new entrepreneurs usually come. Secondly, there are general social influences on the attitude towards entrepreneurship, which are likely to affect the probability that any individual, irrespective of his background, will try to establish himself or herself as an entrepreneur. Thirdly, there are economic influences on the supply of entrepreneurship. These three influences on supply will be discussed separately below.

The population groups from which new entrepreneurs are drawn

Although I know of no comprehensive data to support the proposition, a good deal of evidence suggests that one of the main sources of new entrepreneurs is the sons and daughters of existing entrepreneurs. In less developed countries the largest group of self-employed is the peasantry, and it seems probable that most of the new industrial and commercial entrepreneurs that emerge in the early stages of industrialization come from that group. Of course, this is equally true of other new or rapidly growing sections of the population. For example, most new industrial workers also come from the ranks of the peasantry. Nevertheless, the traditions of self-employment and independence of the peasantry, especially of the more successful among them, are bound to affect the attitudes of their children to the prospect of entrepreneurship. In addition, a peasant family can sometimes give one of its children some financial support; and the heir to a peasant farm has a tradable asset which can be used for the same purpose. Small manufacturing workshops can also be established on farms, as is testified by the history of early industrialization in all countries, as well as by the experience of many modern industrialized countries in which a significant number of small farmers still survive. Governments that have made the most strenuous efforts to preserve the peasantry have usually been motivated mainly by military or political considerations; but a side-effect of these policies has been to maintain a useful reservoir of entrepreneurial talent. On the other hand, communist countries that have collectivized the peasantry and, as in the case of the Soviet Union, have systematically stamped out all independence in the countryside (as well as elsewhere) for two generations, have deprived themselves of a very important source of new entrepreneurs. It may well be, also, that the ruthless destruction of the peasantry in Britain, by enclosure and other policies, seriously reduced the subsequent supply of British entrepreneurship.

A second major source of new entrepreneurs is immigrants. Many immigrants themselves come from entrepreneurial families. This was true of immigrants to the United States from its earliest days, while in the nineteenth century the great flood of immigrants came mainly from the European peasantry. In this way the United States has drained off a considerable part of the entrepreneurial talent of Europe, and especially of the British isles. From the purely British point of view the establishment of the overseas English-speaking countries of 'new settlement', while perhaps advantageous in the early stages, has become in later years a serious disadvantage, since it has opened the door to persistent emigration, especially of more enterprising people. This outflow has, of course, been partly compensated by an inflow of immigrants from other countries, many of whom have become successful entrepreneurs.

The third major source of new entrepreneurs is people who have previously been in employment. But there are a number of obstacles to this kind of transfer. First, much of the experience of being an employee tends to discourage entrepreneurial attitudes. Secondly, the most energetic and ambitious employees are likely to have already attained fairly good, secure, and well-paid positions, which they may be loth to lose. This is especially likely to be the case with employees of larger enterprises. Thirdly, an ex-employee is confronted by the problem of raising enough capital to start his own business. Nevertheless, with the disappearance of the peasantry in many industrialised countries, and the growing restrictions on immigration, ex-employees must increasingly be regarded as the principal source of new entrepreneurs. This conclusion suggests some implications for public policy, and these will be considered in the section on economic influences below.

Social Influences

There seems to be no doubt that some peoples show greater energy and initiative than others, although this pattern varies over time. History records the rise and fall of nations; and in the modern world some national groups display significantly more entrepreneurship than others. There are probably many causes of these differences, including genetic factors, climate, commercial opportunities, language, the legal system, and technical knowledge. But there is almost certainly also a social or cultural factor. This factor may, of course, as Marx claimed, be derivative, merely a reflection of some underlying 'material' factor, such as technology. But there seems to be more to it than that. Even with the same technical opportunities, and with similar legal and political institutions, some peoples in the contemporary world do better than others. It would be invidious to mention specific names; but everyone knows that among the less developed countries, even among those with free markets, some are much more dynamic than others. The same applies to the socialist countries; and even among the group of OECD countries rates of growth vary considerably and persistently.

It seems probable that a major social influence on the supply of entrepreneurship is the general attitude towards enterprise. From Henry VIII to 1870 the English were imbued with a strong spirit of enterprise, which was reflected not only in their economic (and military) achievements but also in their literature. The apogee was perhaps reached with Samuel Smiles' *Self-Help*. For more than a century since then there has been increasing loss of confidence, the origin of which Wiener traces mainly to the public school system.[1] Whatever the reason, the attitude of teachers, clergymen, and journalists towards business had by the end of the 1960s become predominantly negative; and even now it is hardly enthusiastic.

Almost all educational systems seem to have a propensity to undermine the spirit of enterprise. Most teachers are, by the nature of their occupation, not entrepreneurs, and inclined to be unsympathetic to the activities of entrepreneurs. Their natural bias is towards encouraging other qualities, and in particular directing their most able pupils into purely academic work. Excessive concentration on the importance of academic achievement may well be a social fallacy. It directs too many able people into activities that are not productive of tradable goods, while blunting the aspirations of the majority of near-average students. A country benefits from having a few outstanding scientists and thinkers; but it benefits even more from having a large supply of energetic 'doers'. In the creative arts, of course, education has rarely played a positive role, except in teaching basic technology.

Other important influences on cultural attitudes include literature, art, music, the theatre, religion, and politics. Economic theory, and the way in which economics is taught, undoubtedly have an influence on students' attitudes towards the role of the entrepreneur. Excessive concentration on macroeconomics, moreover, encourages the belief that governments can always put things right by pulling the appropriate monetary or fiscal levers. It is often difficult to see the connection between much of what is taught in modern economics courses and what Marshall called 'the ordinary business of life'. Many students, apparently, now leave without even understanding the principles on which the national income accounts are constructed.[2] Some social or cultural attitudes can be changed gradually, while others are more permanent. Perhaps the most that can be expected is that people will recognize the consequences of their own attitudes and behaviour; and that they will see the benefits of making certain changes.

Economic Influences

Any institutions, laws, or regulations which affect the opportunities of entrepreneurs to make profitable decisions can be regarded as economic influences on the supply of entrepreneurship. For example, the availability of good means of transport and of suitably located land on which to establish new enterprises will help to expand the supply of entrepreneurs; while an antiquated transport system and tight restrictions on land use for industrial or commercial purposes will tend to have the opposite effect. The willingness of banks and other financial institutions to provide loans or equity finance to new or rising entrepreneurs is clearly also important. The provision of industrial estates, or 'business parks', is also a crucial policy for enabling new firms to become established. By this means their immediate financial needs are considerably reduced, and they avoid the bureaucratic problems of obtaining planning permission, arranging the supply of services, and so forth.

Tax policies can have a major influence on the supply of entrepreneurship. For reasons explained in earlier chapters the profits of larger firms can be regarded as containing, on the average, a substantial element of rent, the taxation of which may have no adverse consequences in the short term. But these profits are both the incentive for new and expanded entrepreneurship and the most satisfactory source of new internal equity. These are some of the considerations which wise legislators need to keep in mind. The system of local taxation of business property also needs to be examined from this point of view.

A major influence on the supply of entrepreneurship is the availability of alternative occupational opportunities, together with the social security system. The people in the worst alternative position are the unemployed; but many of them are unskilled and lacking entrepreneurial qualities and resources. Redundant managers, technicians, and skilled workers may, however, be an important source of new entrepreneurship. The incentive for those in regular employment to become independent entrepreneurs is much reduced by the good wages and conditions provided to employees of larger enterprises, and by their pension expectations. A policy of allowing employees to take their pensions as a lump sum after, say, twenty years of employment would probably increase the supply of new entrepreneurs. The other implications of such a policy would need to be considered; but it makes little sense that a worker declared redundant after twenty years can receive a substantial lump sum, while other employees are 'locked in' until normal retirement age.

THE SUPPLY OF EXPERIENCED ENTREPRENEURS

As soon as an entrepreneur has started in business he begins to acquire experience. If he is able, ambitious, and fortunate his firm will be profitable and grow. In this way, he will acquire experience of operating on a larger scale, together with the resources to do so. If he wants to, he will be able to expand further. This is the most obvious method by which the supply of experienced entrepreneurs is increased. But, except as a one-man firm, the entrepreneur also relies on the help of others whom he employs in his business. It is often the case that these employees, especially those in the management, come to share part of the entrepreneurial role.

Businesses can be run in an authoritarian or in a participatory manner. All businesses, in fact, combine elements of both these systems. In a medium-sized or large enterprise it is impossible for one man to know everything that is happening, or to be involved in every decision. He is obliged to devolve responsibility for most 'day-to-day' decisions to his staff. On the other hand, the entrepreneur must retain the ultimate power to determine major decisions and appointments. But there can be wide differences in the style of management of different businesses; and much of the success of larger enterprises depends on this characteristic.

The fundamental problem is how to combine strict ultimate control with the encouragement of maximum initiative. According to the Taylor system, which became dominant in the United States in the last decade of the nineteenth century, and spread its influence elsewhere, the best way to make people work well is to put them on piece rates. This system may maximize the output of unskilled or semi-skilled immigrant workers who have no protective trade unions. It was copied, along with all capitalist technology, in Stalinist Russia. But, as soon as workers become more educated, skilled, and self-confident, this system breaks down. Workers learn how to obstruct the system by 'go-slow', demarcation rules, and other devices. The cancer of non-cooperation may eventually grow to a point where the management is helpless (as in Fleet Street) and the only remedy is to dismiss everybody and start again, preferably on a new site.

The alternative is to seek the cooperation of employees and encourage their initiative, by treating them as intelligent human beings rather than as machines. Paternalistic firms have always followed this path; but in modern times the older paternalistic methods do not work so well. To enlist active cooperation in the management of the business, employees need more information, and need to be more involved in the decision-making process. It is difficult to introduce such methods in a firm in which labour relations have already deteriorated under the old system, and where a hostile trade union has become entrenched. There is then a division of loyalties which it is difficult to resolve.

The outstanding example of successful organizational of enterprises by enlisting the workers in the entrepreneurial function is in larger enterprises in Japan. The system involves recruitment of young (male) workers into a majority group of permanent employees, who are given to expect 'lifetime' employment in that firm. For the first twenty years or so, each cohort of recruits moves upwards in terms of pay and responsibilities more of less in parallel. They form a team, in which there is no great distinction of rank, and in which ideas are freely shared and a joint sense of responsibility is created for the success of the work. Towards the end of this period there is a differentiation of roles and responsibilities, with some 'high flyers' being offered rapid promotion, while others continue up a slower ladder. A few of the former group can expect to reach the highest positions in the firm, and continue in work to an advanced age. The remainder, at least until recently, are retired at 55, when they either buy a small retail store with their savings and lump-sum retirement compensation, or obtain a lower paid position in a smaller firm (sometimes arranged by the larger enterprise).[3]

The Japanese system of labour relations seems to be an important ingredient in the outstanding success of Japanese industry in the past forty years. In essence, it is a method of sharing the entrepreneurial role, while retaining ultimate decisions in the hands of the equity owners. The policy of sharing the entrepreneurial role extends also to the relations between large and smaller enterprises. Larger enterprises have recognized the importance of achieving high quality in the materials and components supplied to them by small and medium-sized firms, and also in the punctuality with which deliveries are made. The emphasis on quality has been extended from internal 'quality circles' to placing the responsibility for quality control on the suppliers, while the 'just in time' system of deliveries accustoms suppliers to working to strict schedules and reduces the stock requirements of larger firms. The proof of the superiority of Japanese methods is that they have been successfully transplanted by Japanese firms to other countries, including the United States and Britain.

Even in the absence of the Japanese system, larger enterprises help to train potential entrepreneurs within their own management. The managers acquire the private technology of the firm for which they work, and it may be possible to transfer some of this technology to another enterprise which they control. The group of managers may also take the initiative in organizing a 'management buyout' of a firm which is in decline. In recent years there have been some remarkable examples of the success of such initiatives. This seems to be one of the most promising ways in which the supply of good entrepreneurs can be expanded in a modern industrialized economy.

But in the final analysis a free enterprise system cannot be efficient unless there is a steady inflow of new small entrepreneurs at the base of the system. These provide the 'new blood', the younger people, the people who are not already set in their ways. As in the worlds of plants and animals, the species will not survive indefinitely unless there is an ample supply of new stock, of which only the most vigorous survive the process of 'natural selection'.

8 Some Wider Issues

The alternative theory of competition – 'entrepreneurial' competition – proposed in Chapters 3 and 4 above has many implications for economic theory and policy. In this chapter I shall discuss four areas in which the theory suggests some new lines of thought. These are: the aggregate distribution of income between wages and profits; export pricing with variable exchange rates; the role of government in an enterprise economy; and the possibility of efficient alternative economic systems.

THE DISTRIBUTION OF INCOME

If all firms experience economies of scale up to some point, and diseconomies of scale beyond some further point, their curves of average product per worker in relation to the total number of workers employed in the firm may be expected to rise, then flatten, and finally begin to fall. (The turning point in the average labour product curve will not necessarily be at the same size, measured in terms of number of workers employed, as the turning point of the average cost curve, also measured against number of workers employed.) If we measure average product by value added, we can aggregate all firms into a single diagram representing the variation of average value added per worker with the size of the firm, measured by its number of workers. Although the experience of each firm will be different, the *average* relation in the whole economy may be expected to be of the form shown in Figure 8.1. Here the curve labelled *v* represents average value added per worker, and the curve labelled *w* represents the average wage per worker, each measured across all firms of a given size in terms of number of workers employed (including proprietors).

For the reasons already given, the value added curve will first rise but eventually begin to fall. On the other hand, the wage curve will tend to rise continuously. The reasons for this latter pattern

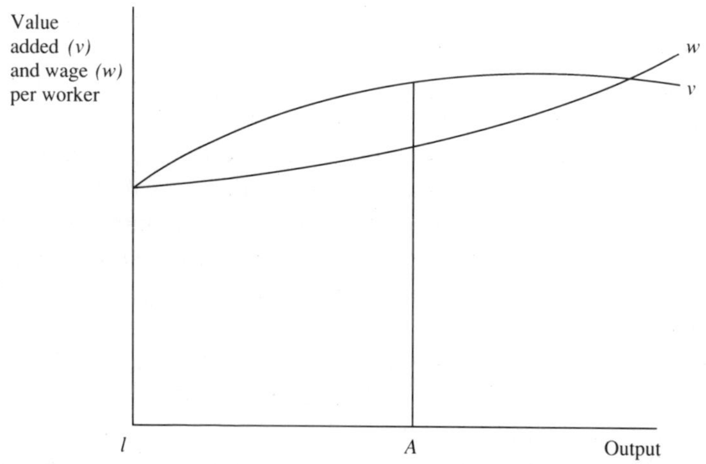

Figure 8.1

include: first, increasing division of labour within larger firms, with larger proportions of more highly paid supervisors and specialists; secondly, the increasing power of trade unions within larger enterprises; and, thirdly, even in the absence of trade union power, the increasing dependence of larger employers on the goodwill of their staff. The shapes of both these curves are consistent with such limited statistical data as are available about the variation of value added per worker and wage per worker in firms of different sizes. Most statistics, when available at all, refer only to the manufacturing sector, and to plant sizes rather than to firm sizes. They usually exclude plants employing less than 5 or 10 workers, and consequently give no direct evidence about the experience of one-man enterprises. In Figure 8.1 I have shown the one-man firm as earning, on average, just enough to cover the imputed wage cost of the entrepreneur, with no margin for profit (or loss). This also seems to be broadly consistent with evidence from the national accounts in several advanced countries, although there might be a case for assuming that average value added in one-man enterprises is usually less than the imputed wage of the proprietor.

If v_l is average value added in a one-man firm and w_l is his imputed wage, the relation $v_l = w_l$ may be regarded as not only an empirically observed (approximate) fact but also an equilibrium condition. Under conditions of semi-perfect competition the equilibrium will be long run, but under fixprice competition it will be continuous. Under semi-perfect competition, if v_l exceeds w_l there will be an accelerated influx of new entrants and, because the gap between the v curve and w curve will also have increased, a more rapid growth of output in all sizes of firm. The accompanying increases in employment and profits will ensure that the w curve moves upwards until the equality of v_l and w_l is reestablished. Under fixprice competition, on the other hand, if one-man firms are, on the average, prepared to earn no more than the proprietor's imputed wage, w_l is the supply price of new entrant entrepreneurs, and larger firms will fix their prices so as to allow new entrants to earn on the average just enough to cover the supply price. For example, if, as a result of public technical progress, with initially constant wages and prices, the v curve shifts upwards while the w curve remains unchanged, fixprice firms will tend to reduce their prices (or increase their money wages) until the relation $v_l = w_l$ is once more established. Similarly, if there is an autonomous increase in money wages, fixprice firms will raise their prices until $v_l = w_l$ again.

The gap between the v curve and the w curve represents average gross profit per worker in firms of different sizes. This 'profit', of course, has to cover depreciation and imputed interest on capital, so that net profit per worker will be smaller at all sizes of firm. Nevertheless, because of the assumed variation in costs with scale, the gap between net value added per worker and the wage per worker should at first rise and eventually fall in a manner analogous to the behaviour of the gross gap shown in Figure 8.1.

In accordance with our discussion in Chapters 3 and 4, the distribution of firms by size, measured in this instance by their number of workers, may be expected to be highly skew, with large numbers of small enterprises and a long thin tail stretching out towards the upper size classes. (This is also in accordance with available statistics of aggregate size distributions of firms or plants.) There may, in fact, be few, or even no, enterprises beyond the size *A* in the diagram. It will not necessarily be irrational for a firm to expand beyond the point *A*, even if its own experience conforms with the average. For a firm in this position may still be able to obtain a higher rate of profit on reinvestment in its own business than by lending funds to the capital market. At some point, however, it will clearly be better for a firm to stop growing, to decentralize its organization, or to sell off the less profitable parts of its business. If it fails to do this, it will eventually succumb to a takeover bid, and the reorganization will be done by the new management.

If the v and w functions are stable, and the size distribution function is also stable, the distribution of national product between wages and gross profits will be stable. Since there is considerable empirical support for the assumption that these three functions are stable, at least in the medium term, it is not surprising that empirical evidence also suggests a large degree of stability in the aggregate wage and gross profit ratios in the business sector.[1]

EXPORT PRICING UNDER VARIABLE EXCHANGE RATES

When a country is involved in international trade, it is possible that the prices of imports or exports will not exactly conform to the theory of pricing under fixprice competition set out above. Take first the case of an exporter. Will he offer his goods or services on the export market at the same prices, in terms of domestic currency, as the prices fixed for the home market? If he does so, he may find that his export prices are either higher or lower than the prices charged for fairly similar products by producers in the export market. There may be cases in which he will allow this to happen. But, in general, I believe that he will apply the same rule to the export market as he applies at home, namely, to fix the export price for each market at the new-entry price of domestic producers in that market, so long as the profit margin on export sales to that market justifies the continuation of the trade. He may encounter some problems of intertrade between markets by agents outside his control; but in most cases fixprice firms are able to take measures to prevent this becoming a serious difficulty.

If the same rule is applied by importers, domestic producers in the importing country will not be confronted by the problem of 'cut price' import competition. But importers that are making exceptionally high profits, because, at the current rate of exchange, their costs are much lower than the costs of domestic producers, will be able to spend larger amounts on marketing and advertising, which may bring them an increasing share of the domestic market. If that share becomes overwhelming, more and more domestic producers will be driven into bankruptcy, and eventually the importers will set their prices without regard to potential domestic competition but rather with regard to potential competition from imports from third countries.

It is easy to see why, under fixprice competition, exporting firms are especially sensitive to changes in exchange rates. Of course, firms operating under conditions of semi-perfect competition are also affected by changes in exchange rates. For example, so long as nominal domestic wages are fixed, a devaluation of the home currency increases the profitability of producers of tradable goods; and vice versa. But fixprice firms also experience such windfall profits and losses from exchange fluctuations. In addition, fixprice firms find that exchange rate fluctuations substantially increase the burden of uncertainty. If various currency rates have changed, what prices are fixprice firms to set in each market? And how are they to police differential prices in different markets? These uncertainties undermine the confidence of fixprice firms in their normal rules and absorb a great deal of scarce managerial time. This probably accounts for the strong political support given by exporters of manufactured goods to the demand for the establishment of a regime of stable exchange rates.

THE ROLE OF GOVERNMENT IN AN ENTERPRISE ECONOMY

Although the main purpose of this book is to emphasize the role of the entrepreneur in economic development, it does not follow that there is no role for government. A market system cannot function efficiently without a sound framework of laws, and without security of individual rights within the law. Apart from its fundamental responsibilities in these respects, governments can assist the growth of free competitive enterprise in a number of other ways. These include the provision of infrastructure, especially of a good road system, and of an efficient educational system designed not only to develop general human potential but also to equip young people with skills that will be advantageous to them in their working life. The government also has responsibilities to limit major adverse external effects, to obstruct the growth of monopolies and restrictive practices, and to encourage the development of public technology through public support of scientific and technological research. In this century governments have accumulated large responsibilities for the provision of other services, and for the redistribution of income. In some of these areas governments will continue to play a major role, as in the provision of health services, unemployment insurance, and public assistance to the poor. But the optimal division of responsibilities between governments and private people in some other areas remains a matter for continuing debate. There is a limit to the amount of government encroachment on economic decisions, beyond which a free enterprise system will not function efficiently, and economic growth will turn into stagnation or decline.

The role of the government in short-term demand management of the economy is now widely recognized to have been greatly exaggerated, and to have done little or nothing to improve the long-term performance of the economy. Indeed, the cultivation of the illusion that governments can always correct weaknesses in the fundamental structure of an economy by manipulation of macroeconomic instruments has diverted attention away from essential reforms. Governments have an inescapable responsibility to prevent persistent inflation and balance of payments deficits, after allowing for a normal level of net inflow (or outflow) of capital. But they do not have the power to prevent or cure unemployment by demand manipulation. Unemployment is a symptom of a poor supply of entrepreneurship, together with excessive power in the hands of alienated trade unions. The two phenomena go together, and mutually reinforce one another. Demand management is like putting plasters on a patient suffering from a serious internal disease.

In my opinion, the absence of discussion of the role of entrepreneurship in standard economic theory, which is reflected in the neglect of this subject in the teaching of economics, has had a negative effect on popular attitudes, especially on the attitudes of educated people, who are still, unfortunately, a small minority in this country.[2] The bias of economic teaching in the past half century has been heavily in favour of government intervention. It is gradually being recognized that government decisions are often mistaken, and that increasing bureaucracy puts a brake on enterprise and innovation. But there is still a long way to go before the respective roles of government and enterprise are correctly appraised.

THE POSSIBILITY OF EFFICIENT ALTERNATIVE SYSTEMS

The only alternative worthy of serious consideration is full-blown socialism. The so-called 'mixed' economy is a muddle, a typical political and bureaucratic compromise in a country in a state of economic decline. The collapse of the whole group of countries of 'real socialism' in Eastern Europe, together with the threat of a similar collapse in the Soviet heartland, has finally exploded the myth that state socialism is an efficient solution to the economic problem, let alone a means of meeting human needs for freedom, honesty, and justice.

The fundamental source of the weakness of a command economy is the suppression of entrepreneurship. The only permitted form of entrepreneurship is that of the Party leadership. It can order the construction of a few giant projects, especially in the military field, and given them absolute priority. Atom bombs, rockets, and tanks can be produced in thousands, but only at the expense of the food, clothing, and housing of the people. The technology, except in the military field, is derivative, and operated inefficiently. State ownership of capital ensures that both capital and labour are wasted on a massive scale. Plant and machinery are not properly maintained and large-scale overmanning is the rule. The environment, also, is misused even more then under profit-making capitalism, partly because some external effects are internalized under capitalism, and partly because capitalism is the only economic system that permits the growth of political democracy.

In earlier years the Yugoslav alternative was presented to the world as a good compromise between socialism and the market. The Yugoslav system, which was created by accident, involved the retention of 'social' (i.e. state) ownership of capital in industry and part of agriculture with a theoretical devolution of managerial responsibility to the workers employed in each enterprise. 'Self-management', as it was called, did not in fact give the workers effective control over their own enterprises (which was impossible so long as the assets were owned by the state, and controlled by the Party), but it had one important virtue. It meant the abandonment of central planning and the introduction of market relations in current transactions among enterprises and between them and the final buyers, whether on the domestic or the foreign markets. The directors of 'self-managed' enterprises, although appointed by and ultimately under the control of the Party, were obliged to look to the market for supplies and sales; and this helped to raise the efficiency of the Yugoslav economy in comparison with the countries of 'real socialism'. But control over investment decisions was kept in the hands of the Party, working through the state bureaucracy and the banks, and led to massive misallocations, duplication, and waste.[3]

While the Yugoslav economy functioned quite well under this system for about twenty years, with much Western assistance and remittances from Yugoslav workers in West Germany, it began to falter in the later 1970s, and reached a state of prolonged crisis in the 1980s. Inflation soared, unemployment rose to ever higher levels (despite an enormous amount of obligatory overmanning in industry), and real wages fell by more than a quarter. It turned out that the Yugoslav 'solution' was ultimately an illusion, like full state socialism. The reason was the same: the failure to permit the free operation of entrepreneurship. So long as capital is owned by the state, or by 'society', enterprise is frustrated, the motivation for efficient decisions and work is lacking, and valuable resources are wasted. These lessons need to be learnt by some who still pin their hopes on 'democratic socialism' or 'social ownership'.

Contrary to the forecast of Schumpeter, capitalism has continued to generate revolutionary changes in technology, while socialism, by relying on routine management, has been proved to be incapable of meeting the economic needs of the people. Capitalism is in many respects a highly imperfect system, and it does not always produce democracy. But it has a natural tendency in that direction, while state socialism has a natural tendency towards dictatorship. It is no accident that serious movements for reform in the socialist countries always lead to demands not only for a market economy but also for democracy. Their only hope of success is that they will encourage a generous supply of private entrepreneurs capable eventually of creating the efficient enterprises needed in a modern economy. Similar conclusions apply to countries like Britain, where the spirit of enterprise has been allowed for too long to languish and to be replaced by state ownership or control.

Notes

1 The Nature of The Problem

1. For technical development in Europe before the industrial revolution, and before the existence of organized science, see Carlo M. Cipolla, *Before the Industrial Revolution* (Methuen, 1976).
2. Milton Friedman, *Essays in Positive Economics* (The University of Chicago Press, 1953), first essay entitled 'The Methodology of Positive Economics'.

2 Perfect Competition

1. The classic exposition of this model is that of Léon Walras in his *Elements of Pure Economics*, English translation by William Jaffé (George Allen & Unwin, 1954).
2. Best explained in K. J. Arrow and F. H. Hahn, *General Competitive Analysis* (Holden-Day and Oliver and Boyd, 1971).

3 Semi-perfect Competition

1. Similar views about the growth of managerial competence with experience may be found in E. T. Penrose, *The Theory of the Growth of the Firm* (Blackwell, 1959).
2. Even such an efficient firm as Marks & Spencer expands its scale of operation only gradually, adding a few additional outlets to its network each year. Presumably, it knows from experience that only by careful planning, and above all by careful selection and training of additional staff, can it ensure that its standards can be maintained. Further examples of similar behaviour by firms are given in E. T. Penrose, *op. cit*., Chap. IV.

4 Fixprice Competition

1. See Joe S. Bain, *Barriers to New Competition* (Harvard University Press, 1956); and Paolo Sylos-Labini, *Oligopoly and Technical Progress* (Harvard University Press, 1962).

6 The Role of The Entrepreneur

1. See A. Maddison, 'Long run dynamics of productivity growth', *Banca Nazionale del Lavoro Quarterly Review*, no. 128, March 1979. The extension to 1990 has been made from data on changes in real gross domestic product and population (as a proxy for manhours of employment) from 1977 to 1989 published in OECD *Main Economic Indicators*, with an extrapolation to 1990.
2. Edward F. Denison, *The Sources of Economic Growth in the United States*, Committee for Economic Development, New York, 1962, and *Accounting for United States Economic Growth 1929-1969* (The Brookings Institution, Washington, 1974).

3. Edward F. Denison (assisted by Jean-Pierre Poullier), *Why Growth Rates Differ* (The Brookings Institution, Washington, 1967), Table 15-5.
4. References in this section are to A. Marshall, *Principles of Economics*, eighth edition (Macmillan, 1920).
5. References in this section are to Frank H. Knight, *Risk, Uncertainty and Profit* (Houghton Mifflin Company: Boston and New York, 1921), available also as a London School of Economics reprint.
6. The English edition of the first book, originally published in German in 1911, is Joseph A. Schumpeter, *The Theory of Economic Development* (Harvard University Press, 1934) and the second is Joseph A. Schumpeter, *Capitalism, Socialism, and Democracy*, first published in the United States in 1942, fourth edition (George Allen & Unwin, 1954).
7. Kirzner has published several books and articles on this subject but, since his essential ideas are contained in Israel M. Kirzner, *Competition and Entrepreneurship* (University of Chicago Press, 1973); references in this section will be made only to that work.
8. The tendency for paid managers to assume the entrepreneurial function in such cases has been pointed out by Kirzner in his *Perception, Opportunity, and Profit* (University of Chicago Press, 1979), p. 104.
9. See F. A. Hayek, *Individualism and the Economic Order* (Routledge & Kegan Paul, 1949).

7 The Supply of Entrepreneurship

1. M. Wiener, *English Culture and the Decline of the Industrial Spirit, 1850-1980* (Cambridge University Press, 1981).
2. See Ruth Towse and Mark Blaug, 'The current state of the British economics profession', *Economic Journal*, v. 100 (March 1990), p. 290.
3. See Ronald Dore, *British Factory – Japanese Factory* (University of California Press, 1973). Also Richard Tanner Pascale and Anthony G. Athos, *The Art of Japanese Management* (Penguin Books, 1982).

8 Some Wider Issues

1. The question is discussed further in my previous book *A Theory of Income Distribution* (Oxford University Press, 1979), Part II, which also contains some empirical data in Appendix B and some simulations in Appendix C.
2. On the disastrous economic effects of a poor educational system in Britain see Correlli Barnett, *The Audit of War* (Macmillan, 1986).
3. For further discussion see my *Yugoslav Socialism: Theory and Practice* (Oxford University Press, 1984); and *Yugoslavia in Crisis* (Oxford University Press, 1989).

Index